Where possible I have used Grendon's (1909) translation of the charms since this is available online so that you can access a wide range of charms, both in translation and the original Anglo-Saxon for yourself.

Contents

About Tylluan Penry

Tylluan Penry is a solitary pagan witch, independent scholar and the author of books on magic and folklore including *Staying on the Old Track, Seeking the Green, The Magical Properties of Plants and how to find them, The Essential Guide to Psychic Self Defence* and *Magic on the Breath.*

She is a popular and regular speaker at various events including Witchfest International, The Artemis Gathering, Witchfest England and Witchfest Wales. She has also given talks for the Pagan Federation, and at independent, private events. Her articles have appeared in a variety of publications including *Witchcraft & Wicca* and *Myddle Earth* and she is regularly consulted by the media for advice in portraying witchcraft and paganism.

Tylluan has her own internet radio show, *The Magical World of Tylluan Penry* at www.oneworldradio.org.uk, and her programmes are also available as free podcasts from http://tylluanpenry.podbean.com/

Tylluan is married, has a large family, many pets, an overgrown garden and lives with Mr Penry, her love of many lifetimes, in the South Wales Rhondda Valley.

Preface

This is a book about the magical world of the Anglo-Saxons, written from the point of view of someone who believes in, and practices magic herself. So although I have included plenty of references to guide you towards further reading, the emphasis here is on the magical thinking behind what they did and thought. In other words, why and how the Anglo-Saxons believed in magic. And to understand that, we have to be aware of how they viewed the world around them.

In school if we are lucky most of us learn just the basics: that the Anglo-Saxons invaded after the Romans left, fought King Arthur and quickly converted *en masse* to Christianity. Then other invaders, the Vikings or Norsemen, rolled in and were fought by King Alfred the Great when he wasn't burning the cakes. Generally speaking though, the whole Saxon period was relegated to the Dark Ages a term that conjures up images of savages living in primitive huts, frightened of elves and ghosts, unable to read, write or do very much at all.

None of this is true. Writing this book taught me that they were clever, artistic, skilled in metalwork and poetry, fond of drinking, jokes, riddles, singing and generally enjoying themselves. I learned a great deal from them.

Above all, I learned that all knowledge is a voyage, and this book can only be a tiny part of that journey. Experiencing it requires nothing more than allowing yourself to dip into the pages on a warm summer's day in the park, or a cold winter evening by the fire. The magic is still there if only we have the courage to reach out and touch it.

Brightest Blessings

Tylluan Penry

Chapter One

Beginnings

W

hen we begin looking for evidence for the magical world of the Anglo-Saxons, we can often feel we are chasing shadows. Even apparently simple questions, such as 'Who, what, where and when were the Anglo-Saxons?' are deceptively complex. It's vital to understand the different types of evidence available to us, and the problems inherent with each.

For example, archaeology can show us the type of houses people lived in, but cannot tell us what people thought of them, or the games played by the children who lived in them. So archaeology can provide only *some* evidence about the way people lived. Also, physical evidence tends not to be very representative of society as a whole, since so much of what has survived was only ever used by a small, elite group. An ornate jewel might tell us what the well-dressed Saxon noblewoman wore, but little about her peasant counterpart. In any society, the poor normally take their thoughts, beliefs and secrets with them to the grave.

With written (especially literary) evidence, we have a different set of problems. Pre-Christian Anglo-Saxon England was an oral based society and their traditions (including charms) were only recorded by Christian clergy. This means we rarely hear an authentic heathen Anglo-Saxon voice since literary evidence was produced by and for Christians. Nobody was really that interested in writing *for* heathens, only in converting them.

The best way for us to try and recover the magical world of the Anglo-Saxons is to work thematically, looking at topics such as charms, dragons, wyrd etc. However even then we must be careful not to go overboard. In particular we should avoid looking for parallels with modern festivals and then projecting these backwards to 'prove' the existence of an unbroken tradition from Anglo-Saxon times to the present day.

We must also be wary of assuming that beliefs from the Norse tradition somehow 'prove' there must have been something similar going on in sixth century CE Anglo-Saxon England. Too much of this results in a lumpy, pagan porridge where Celt and Saxon, pagan, heathen, medieval and

Christian all merge together. In the end it is impossible to tease out the individual oat flakes, let alone see the original barley plant!

Of course, at the opposite end of the scale we should not dismiss *all* later (or, indeed, earlier) traditions out of hand. The absence of a contemporary written record for not prove that something did not happen. Sometimes traditions survive for centuries by word of mouth only. It is perfectly acceptable to speculate provided we accept that proof is going to be hard to find.

Who were the Anglo-Saxons?

Often the 'Anglo-Saxons' are referred to as though they were a single, homogenous group. In fact they were made up of a number of tribes from north-west Europe, including Angles, Saxons and Jutes, who first arrived in England c.410-450 CE. The words 'England' and 'English' probably derived from the Engle, a Germanic tribe from the South Jutland Peninsula. Translated into Latin, Engle would become the *anglii* and then 'the Angles'.

Although few of these invading tribes had lived directly under the *aegis* of Rome they probably would have had some contact with the Roman Empire. It would have been almost impossible to have lived completely separate and apart. Also, in the second century BCE, some of the *Germani* allied themselves with Celtic tribes and travelled south to threaten the Roman world. Renowned for their ferocity, Julius Caesar later described them as *feri*, meaning 'wild things.' Later, in September, 9CE, Caesar's nephew, the Emperor Augustus famously lost three legions in the Teutoburg Forest in Germania.

Britain however, had been Rome's northernmost province for several centuries. It was only abandoned by the army in the early fifth century CE, once the Empire was under threat in mainland Europe, and it was no longer cost effective to maintain such a remote province. Those Britons left behind were a mixture of the native indigenous people, descendants of the pre-Roman inhabitants, former soldiers who had served their time and been granted land in Britain (often confiscated from the native peoples) and those who had become citizens and were thoroughly Romanised.

Although there was no single date when the Germanic tribes suddenly invaded *en masse*, once they did arrive they settled in quickly and established several kingdoms across England. Their power was only really broken in 1066 when they themselves were defeated by the Normans. Even then of course, they did not simply fade away, but learned to co-exist with their new masters.

But why did the Anglo-Saxon tribes invade? If we accept Bede's claims (*The Ecclesiastical History of the English People,* (EHEN) Book I, Part I), then Britain had plentiful food resources, including grain, trees, and in some areas, vines. There were also birds, cattle, beasts of burden and all sorts of fish. Mussels yielded various coloured pearls, while cockles provided a scarlet dye. The land also provided rich supplies of copper, iron, lead, and silver. If Bede's account is true, then Britain must have been an extremely tempting target.

The fact that Britain had until recently been a Roman province was also significant. Any attempts to resist invasion were severely hampered by the effects of centuries of Roman occupation. From the first century CE, Rome had forbidden Britons to make or bear arms, and these were skills that could not simply be recovered overnight.

Another disadvantage was that many young male Britons had been forcibly drafted into the Roman army for a minimum of twenty five years. Sent to distant provinces in mainland Europe, (to prevent rebellions at home), there was little chance they would ever return. It was customary for the Roman army to offer land to retiring veterans to induce them to settle in the lands they had previously occupied. This in turn had a knock on effect on future generations.

Unable to fight back, many Britons fled westwards into Wales and Cornwall, only to subsequently suffer attacks from the Irish. By 446CE the problem had become so acute that a group of wealthy families in southern Britain appealed unsuccessfully for help to Aetius, Supreme Commander of the Army of the Western Empire of Rome, explaining pitifully, 'The barbarians drive us to the sea and the sea drives us back to the barbarians; death comes by one means or the other; we are either slain or drowned.'(Esmonde-Cleary, 1991:137)

Unfortunately there are few contemporary sources dealing with this period of English history. The Roman author Tacitus is often cited, especially his work, *Germania.* However, it was written over three centuries *before* the Anglo-Saxon invasions, and Tacitus was describing people whose descendants *may* have invaded and settled in Britain. Relying on him to tell us about the heathen Anglo-Saxons would be rather like trying to reconstruct life in a twenty-first century city using the works of Jane Austen!

Another author often mentioned with regard to the Anglo-Saxons is the twelfth century Icelandic (and Christian) author, Snorri Sturluson. Although there may be similarities between Scandinavian and Anglo-Saxon heathenism, in his Prose Edda, Sturluson is writing about a different time and place. The Poetic Edda is a slightly earlier collection of Icelandic myths and legends. Again it is often used to support theories about the Anglo-Saxons. All these texts can be useful if used with caution.

Even Anglo-Saxon texts that *have* survived, e.g. Beowulf, the Lacnunga and the Leechbook of Bald, were transcribed only when England had become more or less fully Christian, although much of the content probably derives from earlier oral traditions. It is still possible to tease out some of the original magical thought, but again we have to be aware of the pitfalls.

There is also unwitting testimony about heathen magical thought and practice. This can be found in the writings of Christian authors such as Bede, (673-735 CE), a Northumbrian monk, priest and scholar. His *Ecclesiastical History of the English People* was completed in 731 CE but may have relied on earlier sources such as Gildas' *De excidio et conquestu Britanniae* (c.540). This in turn described events of the previous century, i.e. the 5th century CE, not long after the first invasions.

By the time the heathen Anglo-Saxons began arriving in the early fifth century CE, much of England and Wales was already Christian. There must have been considerable fusion between the various cultures, since non-Christian German, Greek, Roman and Celtic traditions often show marked similarities. This may also suggest at least some common origins, perhaps Indo-European.

After the initial invasion, the Germanic tribes seem to have arrived in England as ready-made communities, bringing their families, religious beliefs and rituals with them. This meant they had no need to make much effort to assimilate with the indigenous peoples since they already had everything they needed.

The Anglo-Saxons conversion to Christianity began around the time of the arrival of St Augustine in 597CE. Years ago it was often claimed that this was swift and relatively simple. Yet early Church authors often complained about the stubbornness of the local people which suggests the conversion was by no means straightforward.

No matter what we may have been told to the contrary, the average Anglo-Saxon was not crying out for a new religion, nor was he in any hurry to desert his old beliefs and magical practices. Despite the Church's best efforts, far more was retained than was ever intended. The clues are there – if we know where and how to start looking.

Chapter Two

Place Names

One of the first places to begin our search for the magical world of the Anglo-Saxons is in English place names. Some are still in use, others are only found in early charters and maps. All of them have a tale to tell.

At their most basic place names reveal something about tribal divisions. For example, the East Angles settled in East Anglia, Sussex was the home of the South Saxons, while the West and East Saxons settled in Wessex and Essex respectively. Other tribes settled in Northumbria (literally 'the land north of the Humber') and Mercia (the land of the Middle Angles, which eventually became the Midlands).

By the beginning of the ninth century, most of the minor kingdoms had been absorbed into the four major Anglo-Saxon kingdoms. These were East Anglia, Mercia, Northumbria and Wessex, and by this time all their royal families had – on the face of it - converted to Christianity.

Over time the spoken language changed too. There were four major dialects: Mercian, spoken in the Midlands and London; Northumbrian, spoken north of the river Humber; Kentish, spoken in Kent and West Saxon, spoken in the southwest. All these dialects have influenced modern English, and even some American regional dialects.

Most Old English literature is written in West-Saxon, probably because Wessex would come to dominate the rest of Anglo-Saxon England politically and culturally from the time of King Alfred (reigned 871-899) until the Norman Conquest in the eleventh century. However, what we think of as

"Standard" Modern English, together with Modern English spelling, owes most to the Mercian dialect.

Given the determined efforts of the Christian missionaries, it is surprising any places named after heathen deities have survived at all. If we look however, we can still find them. For example, the god Woden was brought to England by the Angles, Saxons and Jutes in the fifth century CE. His Norse equivalent, Odin or Oðinn, was imported here by the Vikings from the mid tenth century onwards. The two traditions are similar in some respects, but not identical and sometimes this can be confusing and misleading.

Woden's name often survives in place names connected with great earthworks, such as Wansdyke (Wiltshire) meaning 'Woden's Dyke'; Wednesbury and Wednesfield (both in Staffordshire) meaning 'Woden's Earthworks' and 'Woden's Field' respectively. Wiltshire has Woddesgeat meaning 'Woden's gap' and Wodnesbeorg (Woden's Mound). Woden's Mound also appears in Bedforshire as Wodneslawe.

Other 'Woden sites' include Wensley (Derbyshire) meaning 'Woden's grove', Wodnesdene (Wiltshire) meaning 'Woden's Valley' and Wodnesfield (Essex) - another version of 'Woden's field.'(All place names taken from Wilson, 1992:11)

These sites are not always quite what they seem however. Sometimes it is apparent that 'Woden' sites pre-date the Anglo-Saxon invasion. This suggests earlier sacred sites were appropriated and renamed. This leads us neatly into their magical world. Perhaps they believed that by taking over an earlier site they were also taking over or even increasing its religious or ritual importance.

If so, then it's not all that surprising. In fact it is very much what the Christian Church did to pagan and heathen sites. For example, Wodenslawe was originally a much earlier, Neolithic site whose name we do not know. The Anglo-Saxons renamed it Wodenslawe and the early Church later Christianised it to become Adam's Grave.

The same thing seems to have happened to Wodnesbeorg which had appropriated an earlier Neolithic site before it too was eventually renamed Adam's Grave (Wilson 1992:13). Place names containing Adam or Devil often point to a pre-Christian sacred site, such as *scuccan hlæw* (Devil's Barrow) which is sometimes found in land charters. There are also Devil's Ditches (Berkshire) and Devil's Humps (Sussex) (Grinsell 1936:42)

Woodnesborough (in Kent) means Woden's mound. Many years ago, over thirty glass drinking vessels were found there along with burnt animal bones suggesting it was the site of funeral feasts. These were traditionally associated with Woden (Wilson 1992:13). The fact that early missionaries built a church near the mound also suggests a deliberate attempt to Christianise the site by discouraging people from meeting there for religious rituals. Instead only Christian rituals would have been available there.

Yet Woden's followers seem to have been particularly resistant to conversion. For example, the god appears in the Anglo-Saxon 'Nine Herbs Charm' despite strong efforts to Christianise it. The text reads that Christ (or Woden, depending on your interpretation) invented the nine herbs while he hung, before sending them 'to the seven worlds, to the wretched and the fortunate, as a help to all.' This notion of seven worlds seems heathen, and the Nine Herbs Charms is the only Anglo-Saxon charm to actually mention Woden by name.

The appearance of Woden and Christ in the same charm is intriguing. Like Christ, Woden's Norse equivalent, Odin hung on a tree and both could therefore be regarded as hanging gods who fasted before obtaining something to benefit all mankind after terrible suffering. In the case of Odin, he brought the runes to mankind.

On the face of it therefore, Odin and Woden share a number of similarities and both had attributes that were easy to Christianisse. Yggdrasil, known as the World Tree in Norse Heathenism has no obvious parallel in Anglo-Saxon, but the principle could easily have been supplanted by the Christian cross.

Although we cannot be sure about Woden, the tradition of how the Norse Odin sacrificed himself to himself (Poetic Edda, *Hávamál*, stanza 137) could easily have been transformed as the sacrifice of Christ. Even the runes, with their use in divination (Tacitus, Germania: 10) are echoed by the Biblical story of casting of lots at the Crucifixion. However this particular form of Christianisation never seems to have happened. Instead, of all the heathen deities Woden/Odin would eventually be the most demonised.

In Anglo-Saxon England, Woden was also known Grim, while Grimr was a cognate of Odin in Scandinavia. There are actually more place names in England containing the name Grim than Woden! This suggests either that Grim was the more popular Anglo-Saxon name or that, for some unknown reason, the early Church found it less necessary to Christianise Grim (Gelling

1961:14). As with Woden Grim has strong links with earthworks; the name Grimsditch occurs in eleven English counties, sometimes several times in each.

Thunor (the Anglo-Saxon equivalent of the god Thor) appears in place names such as Thunderfield (Surrey) meaning 'Thunor's field'; Thunderley and Thundersley, (both in Essex) meaning 'Thunor's grove.' As with Woden, we find several Thunor-related place names associated with mounds, such as Thunoreshlæw (Kent) and Thunders-barrow in Sussex, meaning Thunor's Mound .

Other place names include Thunorslege (Sussex) meaning Thunor's grove; Thunresfeld (Wilts) meaning 'Thunor's field'; Thunreslea (there were two examples of this in Hampshire) and Thursley in Surrey all meaning Thunor's Grove. Sometimes names change; an area of old common land at Addington Park in Surrey was once known as Thunderhill or Thunderfield Common.

To complicate things, some English place names containing Thur or Thor are not Anglo-Saxon at all but date from after the Viking invasions (late eighth century CE onwards). It is possible they may even refer to popular personal names rather than the god.

For example, one of the Essex Hundreds (which were administrative divisions set up in Anglo Saxon times) was named Thurstable. It is tempting to conclude this must originally have meant 'Thunor's stable' perhaps a place where sacred horses were kept. To support this theory we could even cite Tacitus' statement (Germania: 10), that 'these horses ...are kept at public expense in the sacred woods and groves.'

However, '-*staple*'could also mean a pillar (from the OE word *stapol*). Even then we shouldn't jump to the conclusion that somewhere there was once a large pillar sacred to Thunor. Possibly it was just a pillar dedicated to someone bearing the Scandinavian personal name of Thur (Wilson 1992:14).

Sometimes place names – or the lack of them – can be puzzling. For example, a number of cinerary urns decorated with swastikas (symbols of Thunor) have been found in East Anglia. Yet the area contains few place names associated with the god (Wilson 1992:17). Perhaps such places did once exist but were Christianised at an early date and their original names forgotten (or eradicated). This is possible since East Anglia was one of the first areas to convert to the new religion.

Another explanation of course, is that the heathen East Anglian tribes simply did not name their villages after gods. Those places that *were* named after them may never been places where people lived. Instead they named manmade structures and landscape features after gods rather than towns and villages.

One things that is curious about Thunor however is that well into the Christian period, he was still being invoked in law-making. So we find clauses such as '...By the abundant grace of God and the gratuitous gift of him who thunders and rules,' (872 CE) and 'inspired with the speech of the Thunderer' (977 CE). Sometimes these have even retained their religious element, so in 901 CE King Edward the Elder made a land grant that states, 'In the name of the High Thunderer, Creator of the world.' (all quotes from Whitelock 1955:499, 490, and cf. 522).

So what we have here is evidence that Thunor was still being openly invoked by law makers and Kings, even though the Christian Church was well established by this time. And of course he (and the Norse Thor) were still remembered in the weekday, Thursday, the celebration of which was yet another practice that the early Church presumably tried – and failed – to eradicate.

Only a handful of places names commemorate the Anglo-Saxon battle god Tiw. These include Tislea (Hampshire) meaning 'Tiw's grove' Tyesmere (Worcestershire) meaning Tiw's pool, Tysoe (Warwickshire) meaning Tiw's spur of land and Tuesnoad (Kent) which may mean Tiw's piece of woodland (Wilson 1992:13). Possibly Tiw was never as popular as Woden or Thor, alternatively perhaps the places where he was most venerated were those that were the most thoroughly Christianised.

Another possibility is that as a battle deity Tiw was mobile, following the conflict rather than being tied to a specific place. Those place names that have survived mostly suggest – like all the other Anglo-Saxon deities – that he was associated with groves, woods and pools.

There are also a handful of places commemorating Woden's wife, the mother, fertility and love goddess Frig, after whom Friday is named. These include Freefolk (Hampshire) meaning Frig's people and Frobury (Hampshire) meaning Frig's Earthwork, sujggesting perhaps that, she too was associated with earthworks.

Frethern (Glocs) means Frig's thorn bush, and this is particularly interesting in view of traditional beliefs about holy and fairy thorns. Other sites include Froyle in Hampshire meaning Frig's Hill, and Friden (Frig's valley) (All from Wilson 1992:21) The fact that *frig* can also mean free may suggest some other long forgotten aspect to her cult.

All the Anglo-Saxon deities seem to be associated with outdoors, especially groves. This ties in with what Tacitus tells us about the importance of woods and groves to the Germanic tribes who were the ancestors of the English Anglo Saxons. 'They also carry into the fray figures and emblems taken from their sacred groves' (Germania: 7), and also 'their holy places of woods and groves' (Germania: 9).

So this is one instance where we can look at Tacitus and suspect that the Anglo-Saxon settlers brought the practice of sacred groves and woods with them from their north European homelands. There is more supporting evidence from Anglo-Saxon place names for grove, such as the popular suffix *lea* and the less common *bearo* (which turns up as Berkshire).

There is much dispute about the presence of elves in place names. Olveston (Gloucestershire) may derive from Ælfstun (meaning the elf's enclosure). Other possible elf-names are Alden, Olvedon and Elvedon, although perhaps they simply derive from the proper name 'Ælf' found in names such as Ælfred (Hall 2006:77).

Yet elves do seem to turn up in some place names in legal documents.   At Welford in Berkshire, a charter dating from 956CE mentions *ylfing dene* (Kelly 2001, II, S 622:p272) which could mean 'The Valley of the Elf Place.' In 1285, Eldon Hill in Derbyshire was named Elvedon, possibly derived from Elves' Hill (Cameron 1959, I:160) or Elf Valley. Elvendon Farm in Oxfordshire is sometimes also called Fairy Hill (Hall 2006:76) Although this is a small sample, it seems likely that elves were specifically associated with hills and valleys.

Apart from places named after specific deities, a surprising number of other Anglo-Saxon words denote a sacred or ritual site. For example, *hearg* is thought to mean a temple, holy place, idol or altar and is found in Harrow Hill in Sussex or Harrow Fields in Cheshire. *Hearg* sites tend to be set apart from human settlements and often form part of natural features such as hill tops. It may be the equivalent of the Old Norse *horgr,* which was often used to denote hills topped with stone altars or sacrificial cairns (Wilson 1992:7)

Often the word *hearg* is combined with other words meaning a hill, such as 'hyll' or 'dun'. None of this tells us which deity was worshipped at these sites however. Possibly gods shared sacred sites that were chosen for their nearness to the sky and that one place could serve several deities. They may have been quite large, and owned by tribes rather than individuals or families.

Another popular component (often a suffix) in place names is *wēoh*. This means an idol, sacred place or shrine and such places are usually found near ancient routes, rivers and trackways. For example, Patchway and Whiligh (Sussex) are both near a Ridgeway, while Weedon Bec in Northamptonshire is close to the source of the River Nene.   Willey (Warwickshire) and Weeford (Staffordshire) are close to Watling Street, while in Worcestershire, Weoley is near a Roman road. Other *wēoh* sites may include Willey (Surrey) which is near the Pilgrim's way; Wye (Kent) which is on the North Downs Way, and the River Wye in Monmouthshire(Wilson 1992:9).

Their proximity to rivers and trackways suggests that people travelled considerable distances in order to visit these places and perhaps take part in rituals there. Alternatively they may have been small wayside shrines owned by individuals and visited perhaps by travellers. However we do not know what these *wēoh* sites looked like nor how they were used.

The early Christian author Gildas (c. 504-570 CE) indicates that mountains, rivers and fountains were considered sacred, describing '...mountains, fountains, or hills, or ... rivers, which now are subservient to the use of men, but once were an abomination and destruction to them, and to which the blind people paid divine honour' (*Works* (II.4). The fountains he mentioned may still be remembered in the suffix '-well' from the Anglo-Saxon *weall*.

Two other place name components, the suffixes *-leah* and *–feld* may have been open air sites under a god's protection. Possibly this ties in with Tacitus' account of the Anglo-Saxons' Germanic ancestors, who 'do not deem it consistent with the Divine Majesty to imprison their gods within walls' (Germania: 9).

Tacitus also describes how suppliants had to be bound with cord before entering sacred groves to acknowledge their own inferiority before the deity. Anyone who fell over had to roll across the ground until he had left the area. Tacitus claimed the grove was considered sacred was because it was there 'the nation had its birth and that there dwells the God who rules over all while the rest of the world is subject to his sway.' (Germania: 39)

Obviously the Anglo-Saxons may not still have thought this way (if indeed they ever really did) in fifth and sixth century England, but it is a possibility. If correct then it could mean that Anglo-Saxon shrines, temples and open air settings, each had their own individual tribal traditions.

However, although place-names suggest some exciting possibilities, they are not a very reliable guide to dating the area. Sometimes existing villages were renamed, both by the heathen Anglo-Saxons and later by Christian rulers. Nevertheless, despite the rather fragmentary nature of our evidence, we are beginning to tease out some of the magical thinking that was imposed upon the English landscape.

Chapter Three

What the dead can tell us

F
rom the fifth to the seventh centuries people were either buried or cremated in Anglo-Saxon England, usually accompanied by grave goods, such as pots, weapons, beads etc. In the case of cremations the goods were usually burned with the body, although sometimes small objects were placed in the urn afterwards with the ashes. Grave goods show a wide range of cultural influences, including Germanic, Roman, and even glass beads from Merovingian France and the Rhineland.

It used to be thought that heathens and pagans cremated their dead whereas Christians buried them (in readiness for the resurrection). However, for most people there seems to have been little difference between burial customs in heathen and later Christian times although cremation was becoming less popular even before the Conversion of England. Also orientated graves, set up along specific compass points were gradually becoming more common (Geake 1997).

By the seventh century most people were buried rather than cremated, and by this time very few were given grave goods although those that were usually had several items. By the eighth century, new cemeteries were established near new Christian churches and monasteries, and burial with grave goods was becoming less fashionable, even for the wealthy. However even then, the Church did not go out of its way to condemn burial with goods (Crawford 2004:89).

Years ago, it was thought that objects were buried with the dead in order to serve that person in the afterlife and elaborate burials, such as that discovered at Sutton Hoo in the 1930's, seemed to support this. For many years therefore it was generally accepted that heathen Anglo Saxons believed that the afterlife continued in much the same way as the life they had known, and that feasting could even carry on underground!

However, it is not quite that simple. Sometimes artefacts are buried without a body, while not all bodies, even in heathen times, were buried with grave goods. Likewise Christians could be buried with grave goods. For example,

St Cuthbert was buried with a comb, portable altar, pectoral cross and a pocket gospel of St John (now known as the St Cuthbert Gospel of St John but formerly called Stonyhurst Gospel. It was removed from the coffin in 1104).

Later, the Christian elite would be buried around churches, although this was not common until c.10th- 12th centuries (Zadora-Rio, 2003). Before that, some cemeteries contained 'mixed rites' with heathens and Christians buried in the same site at around the same time. This raises some interesting questions, since clearly religious belief did not separate them in death. Perhaps at that time, what mattered most was the tribal affiliations that had united them in life. This could also support the importance of a cult of the ancestor.

It is also likely that poorer people were buried with items that have since rotted away, such as cloth, leather or even bread. Much has been lost in early excavations, when 'archaeologists' were little more than treasure seekers, interested only in gold and precious stones! Nowadays of course archaeology has advanced in leaps and bounds and can shed great light on the past using seeds, grains, threads etc., that would have been discarded as worthless just a few hundred years ago.

Even valuable objects pose some difficult questions.. Burying anything means it is put out of reach and cannot be used again. What seems like a good idea at a time of grief and mourning is often later regretted. A good example of this was the nineteenth century poet and artist, Dante Gabriel Rosetti. He buried the only copy of his poems with his young his wife Lizzie Siddall only to have the grave re-opened seven years later so he could recover them!

In heathen Anglo-Saxon times, it's unlikely anyone would bury expensive items that would be difficult to replace without some compelling reason. Likewise burying weapons represented a loss to the community, especially during times when warfare was common. So when Anglo Saxons mourners placed goods in the grave (or burned them on a funeral pyre) with no intention of recovering them, we must suspect there was some underlying belief about the importance of leaving those items with or near the deceased. It might signify that such artefacts were deemed, like the dead themselves, to be permanently lost to the world of the living.

There is also a difference between votive deposits and grave deposits. Grave deposits are just that, they are objects placed in a grave in the earth. Sometimes they are referred to as 'dry deposits' since they could, in theory, be dug up again and recovered (or stolen). Many societies have taboos about disturbing the dead however, so we cannot know how likely this would have been. And although it is often assumed such items originally belonged to the deceased, we cannot prove this. They may have been gifts given at the funeral.

Usually grave deposits consisted of relatively small everyday objects such as brooches, buckles, knives, beads (especially amethyst and amber), spears, shields, jewellery, knives, pots (some imported), keys and cloaks. How such objects were chosen and who was responsible for choosing, we do not know.

Some scholars such as Richard Bradley (1998:8) argue that anything capable of being recovered should be interpreted as a secular deposit, meaning it has little or no religious significance. This line of argument believes that simply putting objects out of the reach of friends and family is not the same as believing they were intended to be useful in the afterlife. This is of course a logical argument, but if true then it strongly suggests that rich burial goods were nothing more than status display intended to 'show off' to friends, family and the local community. Again, we have no proof that this was the case.

Of course, votive deposits were not unique to the Anglo Saxons. Some date from the Roman occupation and also from the earlier Iron Age. After conversion to Christianity, Anglo-Saxons seem to have taken their deposits to Churches, saints' shrines and monasteries instead (Crawford 2004:95).

In today's throwaway age, it's easy to forget that centuries ago even broken objects retained their value, and the act of repairing was itself regarded as a piece of craftsmanship. For example, a beautiful gold and garnet brooch discovered in an Anglo-Saxon Cemetery at Harford Farm in Norfolk, was inscribed, 'Luda repaired this brooch.' A repaired object therefore was not placed in a grave because it had somehow lost its value, but because it was so treasured.

We can see therefore that burying such items represented a considerable loss to the family and community. It is difficult to under-stand why anyone would willingly agree to this unless there was some pressing, underlying need. After all, if the Anglo-Saxons did not believe in any sort of afterlife then the body was simply dead, and had no need of anything. As for the idea of showing off to the neighbours, there were easier ways to do that, such as laying on an elaborate funeral feast. It surely was not essential to dispose of items that could have been used to impress the neighbours for many years to come!

One possible explanation is that some valued objects were consigned to the grave if their owner died without leaving any heirs. Rather than allow the object to pass into the hands of another family or community therefore, it was felt better to allow it too, to magically 'die.' There is no proof of this however, and it remains just a theory.

Another explanation is that grave goods were not so much intended for the dead person's use, but as an offering for those powers or deities who would receive him in the afterlife. In Beowulf, for example (lines 50-52), when the dead warrior king Scyld was placed in a boat with a hoard of valuable items, and the boat was pushed out to sea, we read, 'Men cannot truly say (counsellors in the royal hall and heroes under heaven), who would receive that cargo'.

There is some archaeological evidence that cemeteries were regarded as sacred spaces in their own right, and furnished with religious shrines. For example, cemeteries at Bishopstone, Lyminge, Polhill, Portway, Sewerby, Spong Hill, Morning Thorpe and Alton have revealed small areas dotted with slots, postholes or gulleys which might have originally been shrines dedicated to protective deities (Wilson 1992:48-50). Such sites *could* have been used for magical and religious rituals, although we cannot be certain whether this was indeed the case.

Votive deposits were quite distinct from grave goods, and were simply hoards of objects, metal, bones, pottery etc., that were deposited in wells, pits, specially dug shafts etc. Sometimes they contain some animal bones, but never any human burials and the items are usually more numerous than those found in graves. Votive deposits are sometimes referred to as 'watery deposits,' as they were never intended to be recovered. It seems likely that the sites of votive deposits were regarded as sacred from the beginning of their existence.

Unlike a burial, where the grave goods are placed in the grave on a single occasion, votive deposits often build up over a long period of time. This suggests they were not the offerings of a single individual, but of a family or community and suggests a long-standing, two way discourse between that community and its gods. The nearest modern equivalent would probably be throwing coins in a wishing well or pond although nowadays these are usually retrieved and donated to charities.

Although we do not know what beliefs lay behind these actions, we can make some educated guesses. One interesting observation is that whenever there the number of grave deposits decreases, the number of votive deposits goes up (Crawford 2004:87). Possibly this reflects changes in social or religious structure, or perhaps there were other factors such as famines, wars or plagues, that made people prefer a more generous public offering to the gods rather than a smaller, private one in a grave.

Human Sacrifice

Apart from Tacitus' mention of human sacrifice in Germania amongst the ancestors of the Anglo-Saxons, there is no written reference to it in English edicts or laws. The Church's silence in particular suggests that the practice – if indeed it ever reached England – had been long since abandoned. Bede would surely have mentioned it had it been happening in his lifetime.

However, there are a few curious burials at Sutton Hoo (in particular, the thirteen burials without any grave goods around Mound 5) that have been tentatively interpreted as human sacrifices (Wilson 1992:166) There may of course be other plausible explanations: perhaps the bodies were recovered from battle elsewhere and re-buried long after death. Indeed the shallowness of the graves seems to indicate this, since shallow burial of a fresh corpse would attract wild animals to the site. Also these bodies lack grave goods, suggesting perhaps they had been robbed on the battlefield shortly after death.

Even if these *were* human sacrifices, we do not know why they were thought necessary. There is nothing comparable at the other English ship-burial at Snape, although this is a much earlier date. One theory is that there was a mass sacrifice at Sutton Hoo as a reaction to the coming of Christianity (Wilson 1992:172).

Occasionally, when bodies are found buried in strange positions, people leap to the conclusion that they must have been buried alive. However finding a body in an unusual position can have other explanations. In order to avoid a body becoming a health hazard it has to be buried very deep in the earth which necessitates carefully lowering it into the grave. Usually ropes or some sort of sling are used for this and sometimes these must have broken. Another possibility is that if there are not enough people to lower the body then it has to be tipped into the grave. In either eventuality, there is a good chance the body could twist and the limbs would end up distorted.

There is the same ambiguity with bodies that have been decapitated. Although tempting to assume the deceased was executed, decapitation may not have happened until long after the original burial when the body was disturbed.   At Mitcham in Surrey, bodies have been found with an extra head, with no head at all, or one buried near the feet, and also burials of skulls without a body. They may have been the result of combat or reburial from an earlier mass grave (Wilson 1992:93).

The positions of bodies also vary, suggesting either some social comment on the deceased or some sort of ritual significance. The most common position was supine (face upwards), or lying on its side. Prone burials (face downwards) are often associated with criminals or those who brought disgrace on family or community (Wilson 1992:81). Alternatively burying someone face downwards may have been intended to magically prevent the spirit from 'walking.'

Other curiosities regarding burial...

Although we do not know what rituals accompanied the burial of the heathen dead, the way the remains were treated certainly suggests the presence of a variety of rituals. For example, charcoal was sometimes placed in graves, either beneath the body, or sprinkled on top, especially above the skull or pelvis.   This could suggest that the charcoal was designed to protect the deceased's mind or fertility.

The charcoal itself may have been taken from the remains of ritual fires lit during the burial and the presence of hearths in some early cemeteries seems to support this idea. Alternatively, the charcoal could have come from the hearth of the dead person's home. Very occasionally, the presence of fire marked stones lining the grave itself suggests that fires were actually lit in the grave (Wilson 1992:127).

The evidence from cremation sites is somewhat fragmentary and more difficult to interpret, especially in respect of age and gender. Even so, some of the artefacts placed in the cremation urns are quite curious. For example, sometimes combs made of antler or miniature tweezers, shears and razors were added to the urn *after* cremation.

These are far too small to be of any practical use, and often unfinished, suggesting they were specially made. Many are deliberately broken, thus undergoing a symbolic 'death' of their usefulness. This suggests a magical belief that objects too, have some sort of life. Alternatively placing them in the cremation pot ensured they could not be lost on the funeral pyre.

Cremation urns are sometimes buried in much earlier Bronze Age barrows. This could show respect for the past or even a desire to be associated with it. We have to wonder why this should be, since the Anglo-Saxons could hardly claim descent from the barrow's original occupants.

One explanation could be that burial in an old barrow gave the deceased added importance, i.e. it claimed the same status as the barrow's original occupant. Yet it has been noted that even when a mound has been created for an Anglo-Saxon burial, the size of the mound does not always correspond to the wealth of the burial. Burials in large mounds often do not have many grave goods. Perhaps the burial site itself conferred enough status on the deceased without any need for her to be provided with extra items.

However, the size of a cremation urn *does* often indicate what is inside. Tall ones tend to be for high status cremations, and may contain gaming pieces and even glass vessels, while children were given smaller pots (Richards 1987:136).

Some bodies were simply cremated and interred in the ground without a pot. It is tempting to speculate that these must have been slaves or people without any family to observe the full burial or cremation rites on their behalf. However, for all we know there was a wide range of different practices in various areas over a period of time.

Obviously conscious decisions were made not only whether to bury or cremate, but also in respect of the type of cremation and what happened to the ashes afterwards. What we do not know is who made the decisions and the reasoning behind them.

Of course, material from graves and urns is only a tiny fraction of Anglo-Saxon religious, magical and ritual experience. We simply do not know why some bodies were cremated and others buried, nor why some Anglo-Saxon cemeteries catered for both rites. Sometimes cremations have their own special part of the cemetery, sometimes they are integrated with graves.

Certain trends however have been noted, such as weapons being found with burials rather than cremations, and miniature combs being found with cremations but not burials. Cremation requires tremendous effort and resources, i.e. gathering wood, building the pyre, ensuring bones are sufficiently burned and then gathering everything together, placing it all in a cremation pot and then burying it.

Given that so much effort was involved, we have to wonder why people continued to cremate their dead? Possibly it was linked to religious affiliations. On the continent Woden was associated with cremation and it seems likely this also was true for Anglo-Saxon England.

At Woodnesborough in Kent c.1793, about thirty glass drinking vessels were discovered   near a large, conical hill. Years later, in 1902, a farmer discovered what appears to be a cremation site, about five hundred yards away. The connection between place name, cremation and drinking strongly suggests that funeral feasts dedicated to Woden were being held here (Davidson and Webster 1967:7-8).

Other intriguing riddles surround this site, too. The area where the 'conical hill' stood was once known as Cold Friday suggesting it was originally associated with Frig or Freya. Even the nearby Firtree Hill may be a corruption of Freya's name and have nothing to do with fir trees at all.

Likewise 'Friday's Church' at Wepham Down in Sussex has an artificial man-made mound. This one is topped with large flints, and clay. It had a pool of water that was never supposed to run dry and was dedicated to St Friga (Davidson and Webster 1967: 9). This seems a clear case of Christianisation of an earlier, heathen deity if ever there was one.

Other deities were also connected with death and cremation. For example, the popularity of the swastika as decoration on Anglo-Saxon cremation urns suggests that the dead were placed under the protection of Thunor rather than Woden. Possibly Thunor's association with fire and lightning endeared him especially to people who cremated their dead.

The frequent use of the **t** rune (dedicated to Tiw) on cremation pots may suggest that burning the dead involved invoking gods connected with the sky. The same rune also appears on weapons, perhaps as protection. It may have been that the dead were routinely burned after battles, and thus the link between Tiw and cremation was originally formed.

Alternatively, perhaps it was felt that burning carried the dead person's spirit skywards. Various other runic sigils feature on Anglo-Saxon cremation pots, perhaps as part of a now forgotten charm formula, either incised into the wet clay by the potter or marked later by whoever performed the funerary rituals.

Sometimes cremation pots are decorated with something called 'standing arches' that resemble a line of rainbows linked together. Although it cannot be proved, one possibility is that these may represent an Anglo-Saxon version of the Norse Bifrost, or Rainbow bridge, the link between earth and the gods (Lang 1979:78).

Human figures, rarely feature on cremation urns, suggesting that once cremated, all links with a former life, including any kind of visual representation of the deceased, was finished. If so, then the dead person's possessions could have take on a greater magical significance as a link between life and death, past and present.

There is some evidence that heathens regarded already dead bodies as suitable for sacrifice. After the Battle of Maserfelth in 641, the heathen King Penda of Mercia ordered that the body of his defeated enemy Oswald, King of Northumbria should have the 'head, hands and arms... hacked off and fixed on stakes'(Bede EHEN III:12). Hanging or spearing victims' body parts on stakes is usually interpreted as a ritual offering to Woden. In Scandinavia, sacrifice by hanging and spearing were both considered appropriate sacrifices to Odin.

Scandinavia also had a tradition of self sacrifice to Odin, either by hanging or hurling oneself off a cliff and we can find some evidence of this among the Anglo-Saxons too. Bede (EHEN Book IV) describes a three year famine among the English South Saxons, 'which cruelly destroyed the people.... very often, forty or fifty men, being spent with want, would go together to some precipice, or to the seashore, and there, hand in hand, perish by the fall, or be swallowed up by the waves.'

At first sight Bede is simply describing desperate people driven mad with hunger. However he could also have been describing a ritual of self sacrifice intended to persuade Woden to end the famine. If so, then Woden was regarded as a god who could – if he chose – be persuaded to intervene in human affairs.

However, we must bear in mind that archaeological and even literary evidence does not tell us much about what happened *during* burials. We do not know whether there were processions, what time of day was favoured, nor what was said at the graveside or cremation pyre.

There is some evidence for funerary meals in the remains of animal bones bearing butchery marks. Obviously cutting up carcases was also a good way to ensured they burned quickly, but markings suggest the joints were stripped of their meat first.   The carcasses of cows, sheep and pigs were all of an age suitable for human consumption (Bond 1996:82) However these remains cannot tell us when the meal was eaten, by whom, or with what intention or accompanying ritual.

Horses were also included in many Anglo-Saxon cremation deposits. Tacitus describes Germanic tribes casting a dead man's horse onto the funeral pyre (Germania 27) although evidence of knife marks suggests the Anglo-Saxons killed and jointed the horse first.

Another explanation could be that a horse was cremated when both it and its rider had died together, perhaps in battle. Rather than being sacrificed with its master therefore, both were given an appropriate funeral.

Another possibility is that horse-meat was part of a funerary feast. In 786 CE, papal legates complained that *Christian* Anglo-Saxons were still eating horsemeat, '...a thing which no Christians do in the East (Hunter-Blair 1976:211).

The apparent differences in burials and cremations can also be explained by differences between families, tribes, and kingdoms. Over time they may have developed their own preferences for funerary rites and rituals. This could explain the various contradictions and anomalies not only from place to place but also in the same site at different periods.

Chapter Four

Dragons and Wyrd

Although nowadays we tend to think of serpents only as snakes, the name could also be used for dragons. Nor was belief in dragons confined solely to heathens since in 793 CE the Anglo-Saxon Chronicle recorded 'fiery dragons flying across the firmament.' With hindsight, this was later interpreted as an omen of the coming Viking raid on Lindisfarne.

Even though the Chronicle was written in a Christian monastery, at a time when most of England was nominally Christian, it is interesting that in the same entry, the writer uses the pagan Roman calendar to calculate a date, 'on the sixth day before the ides of January in the same year'. Clearly pre-Christian beliefs and practices were still lurking only just beneath the surface even amongst the clergy.

The Church, faced with the crisis of violent invasions by the Vikings, reacted by declaring that the portents in the sky and the raids were a sign of God's anger. Soon after the first attack, Alcuin, (735-804) wrote to King Æthelred of Northumbria, 'Truly it has not happened by chance, but it is a sign that it was well merited by someone.' He then went on to suggest possible causes, 'Consider the dress, the way of wearing the hair, the luxurious habits of the princes and people.' (Whitelock 1996: 843)

Alcuin is careful to avoid mentioning one of the main causes, i.e. that the Viking raiders were attracted by the great wealth of the monasteries. Possibly he was also indirectly criticising Bishop Higbald who was known to enjoy pagan songs to be sung at his table instead of Christian sermons. (Alcuin *Epistle* 124:81).

Yet Alcuin's accusations weren't entirely out of step with Anglo Saxon beliefs in Wyrd, either. Wyrd was a complex term covering the natural forces of life, or even a judgement or destiny. So the Old English phrase *me thæt wyrd gewæf* is often translated as 'fate wove for me that destiny.' This suggests the Anglo-Saxons must have had a very fatalistic approach to life since everyone including the gods was subject to the will of Wyrd, and this in turn transcended time and place. Basically, to live according to Wyrd ensured prosperity for people and princes, while those who ignored the values of Wyrd were shunned.

The concept of Wyrd remained so powerful that it even turns up in Christian poetry, such as the dream of the Rood, where after the Crucifixion we read, 'I have endured many terrible Wyrds upon the hill.' Although in this poem, Wyrds is often translated as experiences or trials, it may also have intended to show the power of the old heathen deities before the Resurrection.

Ammianus Marcellinus, (Book 16, II:12) is an important late fourth century source of information about Roman Britain, and stated, 'The barbarians shunned fixing themselves in the towns themselves, looking upon them like graves surrounded with nets.' However, in this particular quote he was actually describing the Germanic European tribes. Nevertheless, it is quite possible the Anglo-Saxons brought this dislike of Roman towns with them when they migrated to England.

Magically this poses some interesting possibilities. They may have felt that Rome's decline was due to their offences against Wyrd. If so, then occupying the same physical space (i.e. the towns) might cause the Anglo-Saxons to suffer the same eventual fate. By such thinking space therefore, could be indelibly marked by those who occupied it.

Wyrd was not just an abstract concept but could also be personified, in particular as the Wyrd Sisters. These three women functioned – as far as we know – much like the Roman Fates or *Parcae*, the Greek Furies (the *Moirae*) and the Norse *Nornir*. Nowadays these are probably best remembered as the three witches in Shakespeare's Macbeth. Since we do not have much contemporary information about the Wyrd Sisters, we must try and use these other traditions to find some parallels.

The first sister was probably Wyrd, roughly equivalent to the Greek Clotho, the Roman Nona (meaning ninth) and the Norse Urðr. All four versions show this sister spinning out the thread of life.

The second sister was Weorthend (or possibly Metod) to the Anglo Saxons (Branston 157:71). She was also known as Lachesis (Greek), Decima (Roman), Verdandi (Norse). Usually this sister was associated with childbirth, and with the future fate of newborn babies. They are often shown measuring the thread being spun by the youngest sister and deciding how long it should be. Possibly something very similar also applied in Anglo-Saxon culture.

The third sister was probably named Sculd (sometimes written as Scyld) (Branston 1957:71). In Greek she is Atropos ('without turning'), and her Roman and Norse equivalents are Morta and Skuld respectively. The third sister usually cuts the thread that ends life.

However, it is also possible that the Wyrd Sisters could instead be the Anglo-Saxon version of the *Matronae* or *Matres*, who were three mother goddesses. A great deal of archaeological evidence exists for these across northern Europe, and it is possible that these may have been the mothers of the Modraniht celebrations that Bede says occurred at midwinter. There is no reason why three women could not be sisters to each other and also mothers to their own children. Alternatively there may have been two quite different female groups of three goddesses.

Certainly the similarities between the various traditions suggests either the north was influenced by the Greco-Roman world or vice versa, or that all these images of three women representing fate or destiny originated in a much earlier, perhaps Indo-European tradition.

Although very little information about the Wyrd Sisters has survived from Anglo-Saxon times, they reappear in the Middle Ages in Chaucer's poem, The Court of Love, where he writes, 'I mene the three of fatall destinie that be our werdes.' Possibly this knowledge of Wyrd was been preserved for centuries in folk tales or earlier texts now lost to us.

Early Church writings may also shed some light on the matter. According to the late eleventh century writings of Burchard, Bishop of Worms in Germany, the German people believed that the Fates (almost certainly yet another name for the sisters) had the power to shape a newborn child into whatever they wanted. Burchard's *Decretum* consisted of twenty books, designed to instruct new priests, but it is the nineteenth of these volumes, the '*Corrector, seu medicus*' or *De paenitentia*, that is best known for what it tells us about heathen beliefs at the time. Although writing for clergy in the Holy Roman Empire, much of what he says is borne out in the writings of other English clergy.

With regard to rituals associated with the three sisters, Burchard describes) women putting food on the table, together with three knives, all intended for the Three Sisters whom he equates with the Fates (Paragraph 141). This was done only at certain times of the year, but unfortunately he neglects to specify when these were. Perhaps this tradition was also practised in Anglo-Saxon England, although we lack firm evidence for this at the moment.

Most traditions concerning the three Fates or sisters show them spinning, and this activity was certainly associated with funerary rituals. Spindle whorls are often included with grave goods, especially in female Anglo-Saxon burials. Although perhaps people were simply buried with the objects they had used in life, given the links between spinning and cutting with life and death, it seems likely they also had some magical connotations.

The idea of the never-ending thread can also be found in the Anglo-Saxon/Celtic/Pictish interlaced designs. If you have ever tried to draw a face or animal without removing your pen from the paper you end up with something that looks remarkably like Celtic/Saxon interlacing!

The way that the Anglo Saxons calculated the passage of time also provides insight into their magical thinking. Using seasons and even eons or ages rather than the precise dating measurements we take for granted nowadays, they marked important events with magical actions. For example, the death of a dragon could be used to mark the end of an age. This could explain the popularity of stories about dragon slayers who were later Christianised as St George and St Michael. Possibly these marked the end of the old heathen age and the beginning of the new, Christian one.

As both dragon-slayer and one of the archangels, St Michael's feast (Michaelmas Day) was set on the 29th September, close to the Autumn Equinox. Perhaps the new festival was intended to mark the final slaying of the dragon of heathenism, proof that the old religion was finally dead and buried.

But what exactly was the nature of the dragon? One thing we do know is that dragons were very successful at hiding away, especially under-ground. Traditionally, dragons or serpents (also known as Wyrms) guarded treasure buried in ancient mounds: *Draca sceal on hl æ we, frōd, frætwum wlanc* meaning, 'A dragon must dwell in the mound, ancient, glorying in treasure' (Krapp and Dobbie 1931: 6, 56). In Beowulf we read, 'A dragon who kept watch over a hoard within his lofty dwelling place, a high stone burial chamber...'(Bradley 1990:469 - Book XXXI line 2010-2012) suggesting it lurked somewhere inside a burial mound or barrow.

Dragons were also popular symbols on heathen cremation pots, perhaps to ensure they were not disturbed after burial. If true, this suggests that cremated bones were regarded as treasure in their own right and continued to be highly regarded long after death.

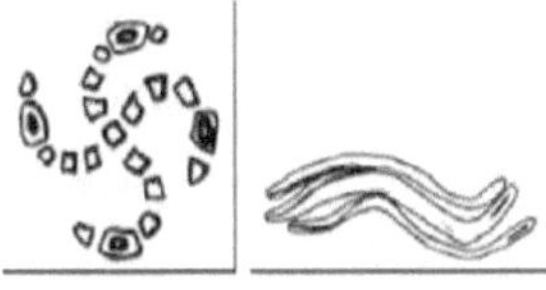

It has also been suggested that the *Wyrm* was associated with the cult of Woden, and possibly was even adopted as the cult's symbol (Speake 1980:85-92). An Anglo-Saxon *Wyrm* looks rather like a snake or earthworm; very occasionally 2 *wyrms* intersect to form a sinuous looking swastika – a symbol usually associated with Thunor.

Even today, many places are named after dragons and *Wyrms* although their original legends have long since been long forgotten. Near Kingsbury in Warwickshire is a place called Drakenage, meaning the dragon's edge or ridge. In Derbyshire, near Burton on Trent, there is Drakelow, the Dragon's underground lair. 'Low' is a common suffix in Anglo Saxon names, meaning a tumulus or mound places where dragons were supposed to live, guarding treasure and – or – the dead (Bosworth, (1838:221).

Perhaps rather fittingly, during the twentieth century the nearby underground complex of Drakelow Tunnels served as a shadow factory for the Rover car factory in World War II and then as a government nuclear bunker from the 1960's onwards. Trivia fans will notice a curious connection here with Norse mythology, since Rover's car mascot used to feature a Viking head and ship!

Dragons are closely associated with wells, rivers, pools and springs as feature in place names such as Dragon's or Serpent's Lane, Field or Well, for example Dragley Beck near Ulverston in Cumbria. 'Beck' was an Anglo-Saxon word for stream, and has remained popular in northern dialects right up to the present.

Magically speaking, these water sources were probably regarded as sacred in their own right, perhaps credited with healing or cleansing powers. Understandably, such powerful sites would need a fierce guardian. On a more practical level, a reliable source of water would also be regarded as a treasure in its own right wherever people wished to settle permanently.

In Nottinghamshire, there is a hamlet called Drakeholes – 'hole' generally meaning a burrow for an animal (in this case, a dragon). It too has a tunnel named after it, Drakeholes Tunnel on the nearby Chesterfield Canal. Even though the dragon legends may be a faint memory, yet at some level their lairs are still acknowledged. In Worcestershire there is Drake's Cross, meaning the Dragon's Crossroads. This makes sense if we think of dragons guarding burial mounds, since crossroads and mounds are both traditionally associated with the realms of the dead.

The name *wyrm* frequently appears in placenames too. On the Gower Peninsula in Wales one can walk along Worm's Head, which juts out into the sea looking for all the world like a giant sea dragon rearing out of the morning mist. Wormwood is not just the name of a powerful plant from the Artemisia family, but also a place in the Peak District National Park and part of the name of a famous prison, Wormwood Scrubs.

In Cambridgeshire, a round barrow in the grounds of Wandlebury Country Park is named Wormwood Hill, while between Hereford and Ross on Wye you will find the intriguingly named village of Wormelow Tump. As we've already seen, 'low' often refers to a mound while 'tump' may be a form of the Latin *tumulus* meaning the same thing. Unfortunately Wormelow's mound was comprehensively flattened in the 1890's.

As we have seen, dragons are closely associated with the guarding of treasure, especially that belonging to ancient, long vanished races. Legends of them sleeping on a great mound of gold is very much in keeping with the 'wyrm-bed', an old kenning or metaphor for gold (Bates 2003:89). This may shed new light on the history of places such as Drakehord and Drakenhord, which appear on older maps.

Of course such hoards were not just places where fabulous wealth was buried. The Anglo Saxon words *eadig* and *sælig* had the dual meanings of lucky and wealthy, suggesting treasure hoards not only contained good fortune but also good luck. Nowadays people often say 'It's better to be born lucky than rich,' but the Anglo-Saxons believed you could be both!

While dragons guarded ancient hoards, contemporary Anglo-Saxon treasure was usually held in trust by the king or leader. Hoards belonged not to an individual, no matter how powerful he was, but to the people. Gifts from the hoard could only be given to someone who had rendered exceptional service to both the king and his people. However, such gifts came with a few strings attached. Acceptance meant that the recipient was further obligated to the tribe. This notion of reciprocity and mutual back scratching is not unique to the Anglo-Saxons, but occurred virtually all over the Roman Empire.

What set the Anglo-Saxons apart however was the belief that the items in a hoard possessed their own soul and were somehow sentient, constantly attempting to return to the collective hoard if they were ever given away (Bates 2003:91). Therefore it was absolutely vital that, apart from the occasional well-earned gift, the hoard should remain intact and undisturbed so that the luck of both king and people would hold good.

To understand the Anglo-Saxon concept of the king's luck we have to examine what sort of relationship rulers had with their people. Most Anglo-Saxon kings seem to have originally adopted Woden as their deity, while at the same time acting as leader of their people's own tribal cult (Naumann 1938:2-3).

In practice that meant the king's god was also the god of his people, and it was the king's duty therefore to act as a go-between for his people and their gods. This included sacrificing when appropriate for victory in battle and good harvests (this latter ritual was known as 'making' the year.)

In Anglo-Saxon England there were three main dates for sacrificing. These were Winter's Day (November 7th) when the king made sacrifice for a good year ahead for his people; Midwinter's Day (December 25th) when sacrifices were made for good crops in the year ahead, and Summer's Day (May 7th) when the king sacrificed for victory in battle (Joliffe 1947:42).

Of course, it was all well and good for the king to be the 'luck' of his people so long as that luck held. Unfortunately, sometimes it did not, and then the situation could prove fatal. Defeat, famine and plagues could all be attributed to an 'unlucky' king who had fallen out of favour with the gods. It was then his duty to make amends, up to and including sacrificing himself. This is widespread and ancient belief, not unique to the Anglo-Saxons.

One major consequence of this practice was that a king could be tempted to change his allegiance to any powerful deity who didn't demand he should sacrifice himself. The early Christian missionaries almost certainly preyed upon such fears, reassuring kings and leaders that once they converted to Christianity they would never again be required to offer themselves as a sacrifice.

Unlike the heathen priest king who offered *blot* or sacrifice to ensure the safety and prosperity of his people, Christian kings were then encouraged to order the *folc* or tribe to fulfil their religious obligations to the Church (Chaney 1960: 213). This fundamental change in the nature of kingship must have been very appealing and we know that at least three Christian kings, Alfred, Athelstan and Edgar who were presented as owing their success entirely to the new Christian god (Chaney 1960: 212).

Conversely, the persistently heathen (and successful) King Penda of Mercia was a rather embarrassing exception. Eventually the Christian author Nennius rather grudgingly concluded that he 'was victorious by diabolical agency' (Wade-Evans,1938: 83).

Christian missionaries certainly used disasters and plague epidemics to help convert the Anglo-Saxons. Bede (EHEN Book IV) describes how a three year famine caused by drought in the land of the South Saxons ended on the very day the 'nation received the baptism of faith, there fell a soft but plentiful rain; the earth revived again, and the verdure being restored to the fields, the season was pleasant and fruitful'.

Sometimes however the reverse held true: a king who had converted and *then* suffered bad luck was quite likely to change back to his earlier heathen beliefs. In 664CE, after a great plague, King Sighere of Essex reverted to heathenism '...hoping for protection against the plague by this means, they therefore began to rebuild ruined temples and restore the worship of idols' (Bede EHEN Book IV).

Although Bede does not specifically say so, his comments suggest that the luck of kingdoms and tribes was closely bound up with religious and ritual practice. In Sighere's case, the king felt his luck could only be restored if he reverted to his earlier beliefs and traditions.

The relationship between heathens and Christians remained complex for centuries. Even though Christian kings, such as Edwin and Egfrid of Northumbria and Æthelberht of East Anglia became popular martyr saints very few churches were dedicated to them. This seems curious, since the Church usually praised martyrs for their faith.

One explanation could be that there was a already tradition of venerating heathen kings who died in battle, perhaps at local sanctuaries, *hearg* or *wēoh* sites. If so, then perhaps the clergy feared that venerating a Christian martyr king would be too close to pre-existing heathen practice for comfort.

It was certainly difficult to eradicate heathen beliefs altogether. One possible explanation may be found in Tacitus, who stated that, 'Capital punishment, imprisonment and even flogging are allowed to none but the priests, and are not inflicted merely as punishments or on the leaders' orders, but in obedience to the God whom they believe to preside over battle' (Germania: 7) Perhaps these priests' descendants had retained such power when they settled in England centuries later. If so, the Church would have been faced with formidable religious and political adversaries.

There is also some evidence of religious belief in royal names. For example, the prefix 'Os-' (as in Oswald, or Oswin) signified 'divine'. It was used by at least a dozen Northumbrian kings. It is even possible, though not entirely provable, that Os may be associated with the Norse Aesir, who appear just once in an Anglo-Saxon charm against rheumatism in the unlikely company of elves and hags (Storms, 1948: 50, 142-3, 147)

The early Church took pains not to appear to change the *status quo* too much when Kings converted and it seems that many heathen ideas of luck and kingship were easily Christianised. In AD 793 Alcuin reminded King Æthelred that everything from victory in war, to good weather and harvests rested upon the King's behaviour, and '...it is for the king to atone with God for his whole people.' (Joliffe 1947:43)

Alcuin, and other Christian authors seemed to have believed that provided the King converted, his people would follow unquestioningly. Actually it was not quite that simple. In fact it was the ordinary people who were to cling onto their magical traditions more tenaciously than anyone ever expected...

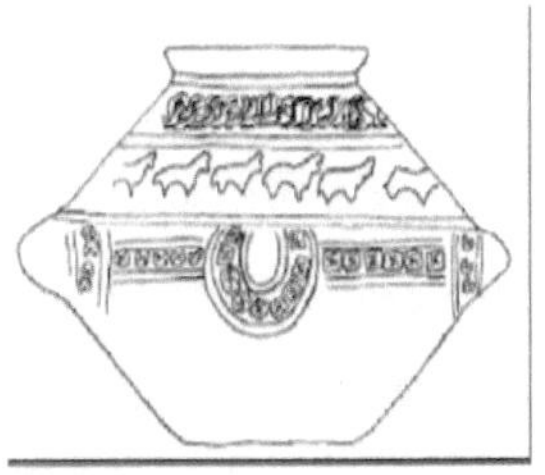

Chapter Five

How they Lived....

T

he purpose of this chapter is not to simply set out how the Anglo-Saxons lived, but to try and show how their lives reflected their religious beliefs and magical practices. Well into the twentieth century, it was still being taught that the Anglo-Saxons were primitive barbarians whose arrival plunged England into the 'Dark Ages' following centuries of 'enlightened' Roman occupation. As we shall see, this was somewhat careless with the truth.

Artefacts are not always a good indication of spiritual life. Often items made from perishable materials such as cloth and leather have all but perished, and until the advent of late twentieth century archaeological techniques, their importance was overlooked. So this chapter focuses on trying to tease out the unwitting testimonies from literary texts, personal names and common words. Even though the authors were virtually all Christian clergy, they can shed interesting light on the heathen period.

Although contemporary Christian authors painted a grim picture of the Anglo-Saxon world it would be wrong to take them entirely at face value. The Anglo-Saxon poem, *The Ruin* (Raffel 1964:27 lines 1 – 6) probably describes Bath in the county of Avon:

> *Fate has smashed these wonderful walls,*
>
> *This broken city, has crumbled the work*
>
> *Of giants. The roofs are gutted, the towers*
>
> *Fallen, the gates ripped off, frost*
>
> *In the mortar, everything moulded, gaping,*
>
> *Collapsed...*

Similar accounts occur in other Anglo-Saxon poems, such as the Wanderer (Whitelock 1949: 93, lines 85 - 87):

> *Thus the Maker of men lays waste*
>
> *This earth, crushing our callow mirth*
>
> *And the work of old giants stands withered and still...*

Bede and Gildas may have believed that at least some of the devastation was due to plague epidemics, '...And yet neither to this day are the cities of our country inhabited as before, but being forsaken and overthrown, still lie desolate' (Gildas in Giles 1848: 313) Yet the fact these events were thought worth reporting at all suggests that plague was the exception rather than the norm.

On the other hand, had England really been as barren and bleak as these and other extracts suggest, it is very unlikely the early Church would have put quite so much effort into converting it. We know for example, from their wonderful metalwork that the Anglo-Saxons were highly skilled craftsmen, and people skilled in something so difficult are unlikely to be totally primitive in others. The beautiful Anglo-Saxon jewels of the seventh century are quite in keeping with people who were already culturally advanced when they reach England.

As far as the Church was concerned, the benefits of converting England to Christianity were material as well as spiritual. When Anglo-Saxon kings converted, they often donated large tracts of their land and estates to the Church. Had these estates been as wild and worthless as early authors suggest, they would not have been much of an offering.

Modern advances in archaeology have enabled the reconstruction of many aspects of Anglo-Saxon life, proving they were surprisingly advanced even in the early period of occupation. Also, contrary to popular belief, they were not permanently at war with their neighbours. It even seems likely there was some cross-cultural exchange with the Romano-British and Celtic Britons.

When the Anglo-Saxons settled in England, they farmed and did well for themselves and their families. They were prosperous and materially comfortable, although, like any other rural society, they were at the mercy of the extremes of the weather, famine and plague epidemics.

To deal with this, ordinary people evolved a complex magical belief system that protected them against the most commonly encountered diseases and problems.. For example, those about to make a long journey were advised, 'He who will travel an over long way, let him have with him on the journey, the wort which one nameth heraklia ... then he dreadeth not any robber, but the wort puts them all to flight (Cockayne, 1864-66: Vol I;177). This paints a picture of a very robust society. Provided the traveller had a piece of the correct plant in his hand, he was confident he could travel anywhere in safety.

Unfortunately this has sometimes been used as 'proof' of the barbarism and fear of the heathen Anglo-Saxons when compared with Bede's idyllic account of the Christian King Edwin in Northumbria. Edwin 'cared so much for the good of the people that, in various places where he had noticed clear springs near the highway, he caused stakes to be set up and bronze drinking cups to be hung on them for the refreshment of travellers.' These were never stolen or broken, not because they feared the king but, '...because they loved him dearly'(EHEN II:16).

Perhaps the truth was somewhere between the two. Yet who can resist this example of a traveller's blessing. It sounds just as valid today as it must have done to the Anglo-Saxons: 'I pray.... for a good journey, a mild and gentle wind from these shores.' (Gordon 1926:91-92)

One problem in reconstructing Anglo-Saxon life is that unlike the Romans, they tended to build in timber, much of which has not survived. So far, any archaeological evidence for a structure specially set aside for pagan worship is rather thin on the ground (apart from a site known as D2 at Yeavering in the Kingdom of Northumbria) (Wilson 1992:10). Of course, if the Anglo-Saxons really did prefer to worship on hilltops and in groves, there will be little to find in these difficult sites.

However, the Yeavering structure has provided some interesting evidence even though dating it has proved difficult. Just inside the east door was a pit containing animal bones including many ox skulls suggesting either a great animal sacrifice or series of votive deposits. The site also contained several free standing posts in the southern enclosure and another just outside the northwest corner of the building. These may have held totems or idols and seem to have been filled in around the time that Paulinus converted the kingdom. This alone suggests that the posts had a specifically heathen role and meaning.

The site may eventually have been consecrated for use as a church, but by 632-3 CE it was razed to the ground along with the rest of the royal palace when Penda and Cadwallon attacked Northumbria.

Along the west and possibly northern side of the D2 site are another line of post holes, possibly the remains of temporary huts. These might tie in with Pope Gregory's letter to Mellitus (Bede EHEN 1:30) which mentions how the Anglo-Saxons 'construct shelters of boughs for themselves around the churches that were once temples.'

There is other evidence too, that the tradition of temporary shelters clearly did not die out with the heathen Anglo-Saxons. The sixteenth century puritan,

Philip Stubbs in his *Anatomie of Abuses*, complained about the early and midsummer festivities involving the Lord of Misrule. He particularly disliked the way hobby horses, dragons, pipers and 'thundering drummers' moved around the church and churchyard 'where they have commonly their Sommer-hauees (*sic*), arbours and banqueting house is set up. (Phythian-Adams, 1975:23)

There is more evidence for animal sacrifice elsewhere too. For example, horse skulls have been found near doorways, perhaps part of a tradition that required sacrifice in connection with new building projects. Horse skulls have also been unearthed beneath threshing floors possibly as an offering to ensure good harvests although some scholars believe this was intended to improve the acoustics in some pre-Christian ritual (Merrifield 1987:125).

As we have already noted in Chapter Four, the Anglo-Saxons are thought to have deliberately avoided living in Roman towns and villas. Yet actually at the time they first invaded and settled in England, there were only about 20 – 25 places that could really be described as urban. Even London's population was never more than about 36,000 (Pounds 1993: 75). Not surprisingly, Christian missionaries seem to have initially concentrated on working in the largest settlements, working outwards and reaching remote areas last of all.

Outside the urban areas, communities tended to be grouped according to farming methods.   Crop farming for example, required large village settlements, the right type of soil, climate and a good water supply. Where possible, south facing slopes were preferred because they provided not only the maximum amount of sunshine but also reduced exposure to wind.

Generally speaking the English climate made it possible to plant crops in both spring and autumn, giving communities a better chance of survival than relying on a single planting. Also the quick growing barley and oats could be sown in March after the worst of winter was over and still have a good chance of ripening in time for the winter.

Because cultivating open fields is labour intensive, a large number of people usually lived together in a single settlement. This group would have included both free and slaves. The Anglo-Saxons are credited with developing a heavy wheeled plough which gave them a distinct advantage in turning over the dense clay soils. Previously only lightweight ploughs had been used.

Pastoral farming however, where animals were raised instead of crops, tended to favour smaller or more isolated farmsteads. Anglo-Saxon peasants were sometimes referred to as *Har holtes fēond* meaning the enemy of the hoar or grey wood, suggesting that they must have cleared forests in order to settle (Pounds 1993:139).

From what we know so far, we can guess that in winter the Anglo-Saxons diet was probably lacking in Vitamin A (found in liver, fish oil, butter, eggs and green vegetables). This deficiency could lead to night blindness, poor resistance to infection and a variety of skin diseases. Charms to remedy most of these conditions can be found in the Anglo-Saxon herbals.

The winter diet would probably also have been deficient in Vitamin C, leading to lethargy and skin problems where lesions would fail to heal properly. This would be a real problem in a society where warfare and skirmishes were commonplace since it could make even minor wounds potentially fatal. Again this could explain the wide range of healing charms that have survived.

Another problem was contaminated drinking water. This was often caused by the process of retting flax in order to make linen and hemp. Flax was well suited to growing in rich damp soil and the resulting linen could be dyed using a variety of vegetable dyes. Unless set far away from the group's water supply, however, the process could cause severe sickness. Of course, not all of us have access to archaeological digs in Anglo-Saxon villages and mead halls. Yet some interesting things can be learned from very small, insignificant facts.

For example, there is the way fingers were named. The little finger was known as the *earclænsend* finger because its size made it useful for cleaning out the ear. The fourth finger was the læce or leech finger and was used in healing. (Clearly this was a widespread practice, since the Romans named the same finger *digitus medicinalis*.) The middle finger was named the *awiscberend* finger, meaning the shame-bearer which suggests it was used for making obscene gestures (but not the two fingered kind generally associated with Britain)!

The Anglo-Saxon word for a thumb is *þ uma* deriving from an Indo-European word meaning to swell. Also although in modern English, the index finger derives from the Latin *indicare,* (because it is used for pointing) the Anglo-Saxons called it the *scytefinger* meaning shooting finger. This would have been due to its importance in pulling a bowstring. If nothing else, this suggests that while the Romans merely pointed, the Anglo-Saxons fired arrows!

Sometimes poetry can tell us about people's beliefs. For example, the Anglo Saxon poem, *The Seafarer* (lines 58-60) suggests that early Christians believed the soul could wander and travel considerable distances while the body slept, '...therefore my mind now poses over the body, my spirit travels wide over the whale's domain...' (quoted in Griffiths 1996:160). This sounds very much like an out of body experience, which is hardly a Christian concept. However, it would be unwise to read too much into lines from a single poem, although it does prompt us to keep a look-out for further evidence.

Archaeological remains often show animal figures used decoratively, for example in metal work. However, is difficult to be sure which Anglo-Saxon deities were associated with which animals. We know that wolves, eagles and bears were traditionally associated with Odin in the Norse tradition, while boars were also associated with Frey. The same animals may have been associated with their Anglo-Saxon equivalents.

Some traditions seem widespread and long lived, making their migration to England quite likely – though not entirely provable. For example, berserkers were Norse warriors often associated with the cult of Odin who wore bear and wolf skins and were famous for their ferocity. Centuries before, Tacitus (Germania 1:43) had described a similar practice among the Harii tribe who dressed up in skins and painted themselves black to terrify the enemy.

Although there seems to be no corresponding tradition amongst the Anglo-Saxons, there is a curious entry in Chapter Twenty-Seven of the seventh century pentitential of Theodore, Archbishop of Canterbury. Here he warns against people dressing up in the skins of animals and putting on masks at the turn of the year. So perhaps this tradition *did* travel in some shape or form with the Anglo-Saxon settlers to England. It is worth considering.

The Anglo-Saxons used a variety of methods to incorporate certain animals into their way of life and their identity. There is a boar's crest on the famous Sutton Hoo helmet while *earn* (Eagle), *hun* (Bear cub) and *wulf* (Wolf) were all popular components in English personal names. Beowulf's name comprised *beo* (bee) and *wulf* (wolf). This seem an unlikely combination, although it may have been a kenning or metaphor for a bear, perhaps in order to explain Beowulf's great strength.

Since wolves, eagles and bears are all ferocious predators the underlying magical thinking must have been that they – or the god they served - would strengthen the person who bore their name or emblem and bring good luck.

The inclusion of animals in personal names persisted long after the conversion to Christianity; Archibishop Wulfstan of York was named (and presumably baptised) with a very Anglo-Saxon combination of wolf and stone. Perhaps the practice reflects the Germanic belief that people possessed an animal double or a *fulgja* that personified the nature or power of a individual or family (Turville-Petre 1964:228-30).

However – as is so often the case - we cannot prove conclusively that the Anglo-Saxons continued this tradition when they settled in England. Going by the way people were named after animals however, it remains a strong possibility.

Much as we might like to, we can make a sharp division between how the Anglo-Saxons lived and what they believed. The two are so intrinsically bound together that sometimes it is impossible to separate them.

Chapter Six

More about beliefs and practices...

I
t is not easy to be sure exactly what the heathen Anglo-Saxons believed. We cannot even prove they all believed in the same things. Partly this is because almost all the surviving evidence was written from a Christian point of view, designed to show heathen peoples as ignorant, superstitious and pathetically grateful for being converted to the new religion. Even Beowulf had been heavily Christianised by the time it was transcribed. Not only that, but it is not describing events that happened in England but in Denmark and Geatland.

Another problem is the lack of any contemporary challenges to these Christian texts, meaning they have been allowed to stand undisputed for over a thousand years. Also we have to be careful to differentiate between the early heathenism of the Anglo-Saxons, and the later heathenism (from the tenth and eleventh centuries) of the Vikings.

Written texts should always be considered in their historical, social, religious and political context. This sometimes changes their meaning considerably. Otherwise, if we are not careful even a famous text like the Bible can descend into little more than a series of sound bites prised out of their original context and used to make whatever point the speaker wishes. (Indeed this is what often happens!)

Magically speaking, some of the most important literary Anglo-Saxon sources we possess are charms found in manuscripts such as the Lacnunga, the Leechbook of Bald and the Old English Herbarium. These date between the ninth and eleventh centuries although they probably incorporate much older information. Most have been very heavily Christianised and retain little of any heathen origins. Possibly the monks who transcribed them felt uncomfortable with the earlier heathen sentiments, and replaced them with something they considered more acceptable.

Occasionally you may hear the claim that these charms never had any heathen content. Personally I think it unlikely that charms suddenly sprouted into existence with the coming of the Christian missionaries. So in spite of all their problems these charms remain some of the closest things we have to heathen texts at the moment. There is much to learn from them and they should not be seen as the sole preserve of scholars, linguists or anthropologists. They belong to us all.

Often, although the words of the charm include paternosters and credos, the instructions for gathering herbs etc. remain quite heathen in nature. Clearly what was said and done were two quite different things. The nature of Christianity also explains this apparent contradiction. Although originally the Church tried to assimilate heathen practices, this only held good if it could do so quickly. As long as the earlier rituals were quickly forgotten and abandoned they could be tolerated for the time being. However, when this did not happen (and the survival of folk traditions such as rag wells and rag or pin trees seems to support this) the Church's attitude hardened.

Even if we cannot read the authentic voice of the heathen Anglo-Saxons, there's no shortage of information about what the Christian missionaries thought of them. Much of this is contained in texts known as 'penitentials.' These were texts setting out in detail the types of sins the clergy may have to deal with in their parishioners.

Although at first missionaries came to England from continental Europe, by the late 7th and early 8th centuries, Anglo-Saxon missionaries were travelling over to Europe. For example, the Northumbrian St Willibrord (d. 739), went to preach to the Friesians and founded a monastery at Trier. Although he did not personally write a penitential, in c906CE, one of the his successors, Archbishop Rathbod of Trier requested that Regino of Pr ü m should compile *De ecclesiasticis disciplinis et religione Christiana* (of Ecclesiastical Disipline). This text provides some idea of Germanic heathen practices in Europe, and shows several similarities with Bede's earlier comments about the heathen Anglo-Saxons.

For example, both works condemn placing a child on a roof or on an oven, and also the tradition of burning grain wherever a corpse had been laid. The fact that the same activities keep reappearing in later penitentials and laws suggests that people stubbornly clung to their earlier beliefs and did not rush to embrace the new faith.

Another famous penitential (often called 'The Corrector') is that of Burchard who was Bishop of Worms in Germany. He produced an early collection of Canon Law in twenty volumes (the *Decretum)*, but it is the nineteenth volume which is of interest to us here, as it was intended to help priests select the appropriate penance when giving confession.

Although he was not writing for the Anglo-Saxons, Burchard's work provides an intriguing insight into Germanic religious and magical practices. The fact that he used so much material from much older penitentials (some dating back to the seventh century) suggests how difficult it proved to eradicate heathen beliefs in northern Europe.

Pentitentials do have a few weaknesses however. They were written to help priests, not to inform later generations about heathenism. In fact, we cannot even be sure whether the writers were referring to practices in the wider Graeco Roman world. Possibly the practices they describe were so widespread that they appeared all over northern Europe. Alternatively, the texts were so widely distributed that perhaps they included just about everything simply to be on the safe side!

Whatever the true explanation, there is no reason to think that condemnation in the Irish penitential of Finian, of those who 'destroy another by magic,' or become a magician 'for the sake of love,' or even who 'deceives a woman in respect to the birth of a child' (McNeill, 1933:455) would be any more or less tolerated in Ireland than anywhere else.

The earliest surviving English penitential was written by Theodore of Tarsus who became Archbishop of Canterbury 665-690 CE. Its attention to detail is quite astonishing. Nothing, from sacrificing to 'demons' to placing a child on a roof or in an oven to 'cure a fever' seems to have escaped him.

Unfortunately for us, Theodore never gives us the sources of his information. However, the text certainly gives the impression that some heathen sites must have been watched to make sure that nobody was visiting them for ritual or religious purposes. If true, this again indicates that old traditions proved surprisingly resistant to change.

Some of Theodore's prohibitions seem fairly standard, appearing in similar works from Ireland to mainland Europe. For example, many penitentials contain standard prohibitions against making diabolical incantations, auguries, divinations, and magical tricks; and eating food that had been sacrificed to demons (McNeill 1933: 453-4).

One interesting – and widespread – prohibition forbids burning grains where a man has died. It's possible this was intended to 'burn away' disease and preserve the health of the rest of the household. Even in the nineteenth century, the clothing and belongings of people with infectious diseases was often burned when they died in an attempt to stop the contagion. Pre-Christian Anglo-Saxon graves have been found where the body was placed on a layer of charred cereal grains (Wilson 1992:96). So here we have a prohibition found in various penitentials right across England, Ireland and continental Europe that seems to be supported by archaeology.

To the modern reader, the idea of putting a sick child in or on top of an oven to cure a fever seems cruel, although we should not assume the fire was actually lit at the time. Possibly the oven, like the hearth was regarded as a magical place in its own right. Or perhaps it was felt that using a warm oven, (perhaps after the baking was finished), was a case of *similia similibus curantur* or 'like cures like.'

Therefore placing a child in or on a warm place may have been thought to magically 'draw out' a fever. Although individual domestic ovens were rare even in early Victorian homes, the Anglo-Saxon settlement at West Stowe has revealed the remains of large clay covered baking ovens so such magical practices could have involved the whole community rather than just a few individuals.

Of course many non-Christian cultures – not just the Anglo-Saxons – recognised the importance of bread and cereal grains, especially as an offering to the souls of the dead. We also know from the various penitentials and also some of the Anglo-Saxon Charms that bread was used in magic. Perhaps the fact that the practice was so widespread explains why the Church found it so hard to eradicate and eventually resorted to stamping loaves with Christian symbols (for example, Hot Cross Buns although they may also represent the pre-Christian sun wheel symbol.)

In his work 'Of Greed and Other Vices' (McNeill 1933:454), Bede warns against 'those who practice auguries and divinations' and 'those who let loose tempests.' This strongly suggests the Anglo-Saxons practised weather magic. Storms are, after all, part of everyday life and the Anglo-Saxon god Thunor was a god of storms.

One reason why the early Church found it so difficult to eradicate weather magic may have been because the clergy were doing much the same thing themselves. Although Bede condemned heathens who raised storms, in his *Life and Miracles of St Cuthbert, Bishop of Lindisfarne,* (c.720 CE) he clearly approves when the seventh century saint prays and causes the storm to subside (EHEN: III). We see these dual standards time and again in the ancient texts: magic in the hands of the clergy was acceptable, whereas magic in the hands of ordinary people (whether or not they were heathens) was not.

For example, the Christogram (the entwined letters IHS) is usually thought to stand for Iesus Hominum Salvator meaning Jesus, saviour of men. As late as the Middle Ages, Christograms were considered a perfectly acceptable part of the official art and iconography of the Christian Church all over Europe. However the same symbol could be used to create amulets or phylacteries on papyri or golden *lamellae* that were then rolled up and worn about the person (Maguire 1997:1038). This practice was roundly condemned by the Church.

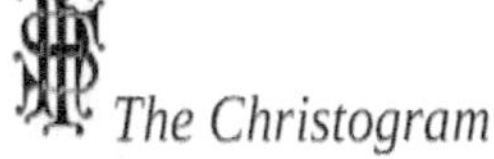 *The Christogram*

What this tells us is that that just because an image or practice *appears* Christian to us nowadays, it may not have had the same meaning centuries ago. Meanings – and interpretations – are always changing even when the symbol stays the same.

The Church also regularly condemned people who took or released vows at trees or anywhere other than in a church. This practice was extremely widespread and there were 'god oaks' sacred to Thor, Thunor and Donar, all over northern Europe. Early missionaries took it upon themselves to systematically destroy such trees. Even the English-born St Boniface took up his axe and personally cut down the Donar Oak at Gaesmere in Central Germany, (c.723 CE) just a few years before Bede completed his *The Ecclesiastical History of the English People* (Talbot 1954:10). Half a century later, in 772CE, the Emperor Charlemagne destroyed a great tree venerated by the European Saxons. This had been named Irminshul and local people believed it supported the universe (Wilson 1992:42).

Although we lack similar stories concerning similar 'god oaks' in England, they may well have existed if the place names associating Thunor and trees are anything to go by. The charter bounds of Taunton in Somerset refer to the '...ash tree which the ignorant call sacred.' (Turner 2006:131) It seems likely that some trees were singled out for veneration perhaps due to size, age or legends that are now lost to us.

The Church also prohibited people from eating or drinking in any areas that had been sacred to heathen or pagan deities. This suggests that food had at one time been an intrinsic part of these early rituals.

Another thing we can infer from the penitentials, is the Church's determination to prevent people doing anything of a religious or ritual nature in private. In public of course, the clergy would always be present, controlling what people did and said. Slowly just about everything people believed and thought was slowly being brought under Church scrutiny and control. Private rituals made such interference impossible, and therefore the Church focused on trying to eradicate them.

Sometimes however there is a flash of unintentional humour in the penitentials and we cannot help wonder what sort of parishioners Burchard and his clergy thought they were dealing with. For example, he instructs priests to ask, 'Have you mixed any lethal potion and killed anyone with it?' (Paragraph 153) while paragraph 124 asks, 'Have you burned down a church or approved of this?' Perhaps there was considerably more violent resistance to Christianity in Northern Europe than we realise.

Things were little better even during church services. Burchard (Paragraph 133) describes priests struggling to make themselves heard above the talk and gossip of the congregations. Even when the 'priest greets them and calls them to prayer, they return to their stories and say no responses or prayers.'

Naturally, the Church was unlikely to publicise such difficulties to all and sundry. The penitentials after all were intended to be read only by the clergy. Yet even these brief glimpses suggest people only attended church because they had to and not because they felt any spiritual calling. Little wonder so many heathen traditions continued for centuries after the Church claimed to have eradicated them.

Bede 's (EHEN I: 25) account of how Augustine first landed in England in 597CE, and set out to visit Æthelbert, the Saxon King of Kent contains an interesting comment. Instead of inviting the visitor into his home, the king took the unusual precaution of setting up camp on an island, meeting Augustine and his missionary companions out in the open, '...lest, according to an ancient superstition, if they practiced any magical arts they might impose upon him, and so get the better of him.'

Reading this, we have to ask why people would feel safer out of doors. There was certainly no lack of protective magic, the Anglo-Saxon charms are full of instructions for protecting oneself against all sorts of sorcery. Possibly the

Anglo-Saxons believed the spirits of the land or elements would protect them. Or that certain types of magic were more concentrated within four walls. We do not know exactly what the 'ancient superstition' was, but somehow it resulted in a difference between magic practised indoors and outside.

According to Bede, Augustine swiftly converted Æthelbert and his people. They then attended a conference on the borders of the Wiccii and West Saxons at a place that became known as Augustine's Ac, meaning Augustine's Oak (EHEN II:2). This suggests by then Augustine understood that people felt more comfortable meeting him in an outdoor location. Also, as we have already seen, the god Thunor was traditionally worshipped beneath an Oak tree. Instead of felling a long-standing sacred tree, Augustine had it renamed and thus Christianised. This allowed him to claim authority not only from the Church but also from earlier, heathen traditions.

Shortly after Augustine's arrival, Pope Gregory the Great wrote to Bishop Mellitus with a list of instructions for the conversion of England in 601CE. In particular he recommended that Christian missionaries should take over what they could of the pre-existing heathen beliefs, advising, '...the temples of the idols in that nation ought not to be destroyed' (Bede EHEN I:30). It seems likely Augustine had already had much the same idea.

Still later, in 684 CE - by which time England was officially Christian - the Church still held meetings in areas that must once have been regarded as sacred by the heathens. A synod attended by Cuthbert, Archbishop Theodore and King Egfrid, was held near the river Alne at a place called Twyford, meaning two fords. The river Alne takes its name from the Celtic *alwen*, meaning bright or shining (possibly an equivalent of the Anglo-Saxon elf!)

It may seem surprising that Christian leaders held important meetings out of doors in areas that had once held spiritual significance for heathen Celts and Anglo-Saxons. This particular meeting, intended to appoint Cuthbert as bishop of the church of Lindisfarne, could surely have been held in an ecclesiastical building. The thinking behind this must have been that by taking over such sites allowed the Church to claim spiritual authority even over those who did not share their religious beliefs. Also, the sites were removed from heathen jurisdiction.

According to the surviving literary texts, the conversion to Christianity happened very quickly. This success is often credited to Pope Gregory's caution, perhaps because he realised that more aggressive methods would be counter-productive. It may also have been felt it would be easier to persuade people to visit sites and buildings they already regarded as sacred.

Gregory's advice to retain heathen religious buildings, '...if those temples are well built' (EHEN I:30) implies that by the early seventh century, the Anglo-Saxons were no longer only worshipping in outdoor groves or shrines. However, archaeological evidence for their shrines and temples is sparse although there are a handful of exceptions. At Bishopstone in Sussex, for example, the remains of a building tentatively identified as a heathen shrine (Laing 1979) were discovered in an area of the church cemetery where there were no burials. The presence of the nearby Christian church may indicate that the heathen shrine was subsequently taken over.

Although few and far between, these findings do not seem to agree with Tacitus' early account of the Germanic tribes worshipping only out of doors in wooded groves. Possibly, by the time the Anglo-Saxons arrived in England their practices had changed slightly. Possibly a difference in climate made covered, solid buildings more appealing. Or perhaps the Anglo-Saxons copied the idea of religious buildings from the Romans; we simply cannot be sure at this point. It is also possible they built artificial sacred groves; a site at Blacklow Hill (Warwickshre) contains 270 circular pits, plus slots cut into sandstone bedrock and fifty two rectangular post holes (Wilson 1992:64).

While Pope Gregory was prepared to assimilate heathen temples and shrines, he was opposed to preserving any images or idols within them and instructed, 'Let the idols that are in them be destroyed; let holy water be made and sprinkled in the said temples.' (EHEN I:30)

These instructions suggest the Anglo-Saxons kept *something* in their temples although we do not know what these items might have been or how they were used. We should not assume they kept physical images of their deities or totem animals. It is even possible the Pope was simply applying what he already knew of Roman pagan practices and assuming all non-Christians did the same.

However, Bede (our source for Gregory's instructions) was not only Northumbrian born and bred, but also highly educated and intelligent. It seems unlikely – though not impossible – that he could confuse local heathen beliefs with classical paganism. When he writes about idols being destroyed therefore it seems likely he is telling the truth.

Gregory provides us with a few more clues too. For example, he instructs, 'Let altars be erected and relics placed. And because they have been used to slaughter many oxen in the sacrifices to devils, some solemnity must be substituted for them on this account.' (EHEN I:30)

In many traditions, animals were sacrificed at an altar, and here Gregory is implying this was also the case with the heathen Anglo-Saxons. It is not clear however whether he intended the old altars to be removed and replaced with new ones, or simply purified and then re-used. If they were capable of being re-used then this suggests they must have been similar in shape and size to Christian altars of the period.

From the modern point of view of course, we notice that Gregory never condemns killing animals as part of a religious ritual, only requires it was done '...to the praise of God in their eating, and returning thanks to the Giver of all things for their sustenance.' (EHEN I:30) Clearly the early Church was not that concerned about animal sacrifice, only that such offerings were made to the Christian God and not heathen deities.

Bede tells us a little more about heathen altars in his account of King Redwald of Kent (EHEN II: 15). Redwald became notorious because he converted to Christianity and then reverted back to his old beliefs. He is often claimed to be the King commemorated in the magnificent ship burial at Sutton Hoo.

Unlike some of the other Anglo-Saxon Kings (such as King Edwin of Northumbria) Redwald's wife was not Christian. Bede states that Redwald, '...on his return home... was seduced by his wife and certain perverse teachers, and turned back from the sincerity of the faith.' It could be argued that since Redwald became a Christian when he was away from home before reverting on his return, this shows the tremendous pressure the early Church must have applied in order to persuade him to convert. Equally of course, the Church would have argued that it was Redwald's wife who was applying unreasonable pressure!

After his reversion, Redwald must have tried to hedge his spiritual bets. Bede states, '...he seemed at the same time to serve Christ and the gods whom he had served before; and in the same temple he had an altar to sacrifice to Christ, and another small one to offer victims to devils'. This suggests Redwald did not completely turn his back on Christianity but tried to keep something of each faith side by side. The idea of sacrificing to several deities within the same physical space was probably acceptable as far as heathenism was concerned. Christianity however, being monotheistic, would not tolerate this.

Yet it was the Anglo-Saxons' spiritual flexibility that allowed so much of their heathenism to continue, even when outwardly conforming to the new faith. Their magical world continued even as their shrines were being built over. The Church may have thought it had triumphed. The reality however was somewhat different.

Chapter Seven

The Resistance to Christianity

R

eading the early sources, it would be easy to assume that the changeover from heathenism to Christianity was smooth and straightforward. Yet time and again we read that whenever danger threatened, the people quickly reverted to their previous beliefs and turned their back on Christianity (Bede EHEN IV: 27).

Apart from Redwald (mentioned in the previous chapter) several other prominent converts reverted to heathenism, including Eadbald (son of King Æthelbert of Kent and Essex) and the sons of the Saberht, the Christian King of the East Saxons. Indeed, Saberht's heirs not only reverted to heathenism but also forcibly ejected the Bishops. Nor was this simply the brief action of one or two men. Even when the heirs died, Bede writes, 'The people, having been once turned to wickedness, though the authors of it were destroyed, would not be corrected, nor return to the unity of faith and charity.' (EHEN II:5).

The problem seems to have been widespread. In London the people refused to receive Bishop Mellitus, preferring '...to be under their idolatrous high priests.'(Bede EHEN II: 6). Bede blamed their King, Eadbald of Kent, accusing him of being too weak to '...restore the bishop to his church against the will and consent of the pagans.' The real problem seems to have been that the Church overestimated the King's power and underestimated that of his people.

Occasionally, local people were not afraid to show outright hostility. In *The Life and Miracles of St. Cuthbert, Bishop of Lindesfarne* (written c721 CE) (Chapter 3) Bede describes how a group of monks were caught in a storm at the mouth of the river Tyne. While they prayed for safety, local people standing nearby declared it was a punishment for the monks '...abandoning the usual modes of life, and framing for themselves new rules by which to guide their conduct.'

Their hostility was so implacable, they declared, 'Nobody shall pray for them: may God spare none of them for they have taken away from men the ancient rites and customs.' Obviously Bede needed to show how Cuthbert overcame the storm and saved the monks, but he also inadvertently shows the strength of local resentment towards the new faith and its missionaries.

Although it is often claimed that the whole of England was more or less Christian by the time the Synod of Whitby took place in 664CE, this seems unlikely. Years later Bede was complaining how people resorted to '...enchantments, spells, or other secrets of the hellish art.' The first Anglo-Saxon ruler to formally outlaw heathenism was Æthelbert's grandson, King Eorcenberht of Kent in 640 CE. Yet by the end of the seventh century his successor King Wihtred still found himself having to make laws that forbade forbid freemen and slaves from making 'offerings to devils' (Chaney 1960: 198). This suggests that Anglo-Saxon heathen beliefs were not only steeped in magic and charms but were persistent, common knowledge. In this respect an oral-based tradition could be extremely difficult to eradicate.

Even charismatic preachers such as Paulinus often struggled against their own clergy's backsliding. When Edwin wished to marry the Christian daughter of King Æthelbert of Kent, Paulinus accompanied her, perhaps hoping to convert her new husband. However, he even had his work cut out, 'to retain those that went with him, that they should not revolt from the faith...'(Bede EHEN Book II: 9).

From this we can see that the popular view of everyone welcoming Christianity is simply not true. Finally even Paulinus was forced to admit defeat, with Bede wearily blaming, 'the god of this world... [who] ... blinded the minds of them that believed not.' (Here Bede is actually quoting from the New Testatment, II Corinthians 4.4).

The heathen practices and beliefs of the Anglo-Saxons took a long time to die out, if indeed they ever really did. Rulers such as Alfred, Edward the Elder, Æthelstan, Edmund, Æthelred the Redeless (also known as Ethelred the Unready) and Cnut all had to pass laws against heathenism and heathen practices. Time and again we encounter harsh penalties for workers of *lyblac* (sorcery or magic), witches, diviners, and morth-workers (usually associated with the occult) showing how these aspects of Anglo-Saxon heathenism persisted long after the Church claimed to have converted everyone.

Barely a century before the Battle of Hastings, Abbot Ælfric was warning his flock not to 'enquire of the foul witch concerning his health, though she may be able to tell something through the Devil' (Skeat, 1881 Book VII, 373:line

126).   It is a revealing comment, telling us not only that 'witches' still existed, but that they were active and accurate in their predictions!

In the same text, Ælfric also complains of people bringing 'their offerings to an earth-fast stone, and eke to trees, and to well-springs, even as witches teach.' This shows two things – a long tradition of outdoor ritual, and that 'witches' (we really have little idea exactly what Ælfric meant here) undertook teaching and training. Clearly the Church was not finding it easy to suppress any of this.

Even famous accounts of successful conversions can bear unwitting testimony. According to Bede, (EHEN II: 13), when King Edwin of Northumbria was under pressure to convert to Christianity in 627 CE, he held a council to advise him. His chief priest, a man called Coifi suddenly announced that the old heathen religion '...has, as far as I can learn, no virtue in it.'

Often people pounce upon this quote as somehow 'proving' that heathenism had run its course and people were tired of it. However Bede is rather coy with his information. We do not know for sure whether there was any hierarchy within the heathen priesthood, and bearing in mind that at this point Coifi himself was still an unbaptised heathen, his surprising response must make us wonder what else could have been going on behind the scenes.

If we read on, the story becomes even more intriguing. Coifi explains, 'For none of your people has applied himself more diligently to the worship of our gods than I; and yet there are many who receive greater favours from you, and are more preferred than I, and who are more prosperous in all their undertakings.' This seems to be less about religion and more the sentiments of a man who feels hard done by. In fact it sounds as though one of the missionaries, possibly Paulinus himself since he was already spiritual advisor to Edwin's wife, had sown the seeds of jealousy in Coifi's mind.

Reading between the lines, we can almost hear the whispering, '...*why haven't your gods made the king reward you properly?*' In fact these are almost Coifi's exact words, 'If the gods were good for anything, they would rather forward me who has been more careful to serve them.'

Next, Coifi asked to hear Paulinus preach. It is this request more than anything else so far that should alert our suspicions. By asking to hear Paulinus preach, Coifi would be able to deny being bought off, since he could always claim to have been swayed by the power of the arguments. Perhaps

Paulinus had promised he would increase Coifi's influence and authority if only he would encourage the King's conversion.

Coifi then announced that everyone should 'instantly abjure and set fire to those temples and altars which we have consecrated without reaping any benefits from them.' These temples sound like real structures, probably wooden, because these would burn more easily than stone. Coifi also implies that heathens habitually performed rituals of consecration in or at their sacred buildings.

What is most surprising about this account is how readily King Edwin agreed to 'profane the altars and temples of their idols, with the enclosures that were about them.' This is quite at odds with Pope Gregory's earlier attempts at quietly taking over the heathen temples without alienating local people.

Bede's account also reveals that the heathen altars and temples were accompanied by statues and surrounded by some sort of enclosure. This seems to support Tacitus' much earlier claim (Germania Book 1: vii) that the Germanic tribes possessed 'figures and images taken from their sacred groves'. Of course we cannot know whether the Anglo-Saxons brought such traditions with them or whether it was something that developed once they settled here, perhaps influenced by Romano-British temples.

Coifi's role in Northumbria's conversion was not quite over. He then asked Edwin to 'furnish him with arms and a stallion'. He then rode out to 'destroy the idols; for it was not lawful before for the high priest either to carry arms or to ride on any but a mare'. This suggests there were certain restrictions on what heathen priests were allowed to do.

Having mounted the King's horse, Coifi strapped on a sword, picked up a spear and rode off to the temple. Local people 'concluded he was distracted' implying they had no idea what had been happening and had not been present at the Council. Clearly at this stage Coifi must have been acting alone, otherwise Bede would have gleefully recorded him riding with a band of supporters (although later he is mentioned as having companions).

When Coifi approached the temple, 'he profaned the same, casting into it the spear which he held'. Although the names of the temple's gods are never mentioned, Woden was probably one of them since hurling spears and lighting fires were traditionally associated with his sacrificial rites (Davidson 1973: 51). Before battle, warriors often threw a spear over the heads of opposing armies as a way of claiming them for Woden.

Coifi then 'commanded his companions to destroy the temple, with all its enclosures, by fire' implying there was enough wood either in or near in these buildings for them to burn. Bede states simply that Coifi 'profaned and destroyed the altars which he had himself consecrated.' Reading between the lines, this suggests consecration was a well established heathen ritual.

Although we cannot be certain of the exact location of Coifi's temple, it is usually thought to have been the site of the present day Church, All Saints or All Hallows near Goodmanham, Yorkshire. Not far away lies the village of Market Weighton, whose name may derive from *weog* meaning an idol or hill shrine. Edwin and his people are believed to have formally converted at his palace at Yeavering, which had been a sacred site since Neolithic times.

In his dramatic account of Edwin's conversion and Coifi's defection, Bede also includes a contribution by an unnamed man. This vividly shows the Anglo-Saxon mindset. 'The present life of man, O king, seems to me, in comparison with that time which is unknown to us, like to the swift flight of a sparrow through the room wherein you sit at supper in winter amid your officers and ministers, with a good fire in the midst whilst the storms of rain and snow prevail abroad; the sparrow, I say, flying in at one door and immediately another, whilst he is within is safe from the wintry but after a short space of fair weather he immediately vanishes out of your sight into the dark winter from which he has emerged. So this life of man appears for a short space but of what went before or what is to follow' (EHEN II:13).

Anyone who has ever sat in a large, draughty building on a winter's evening and seen a small bird briefly fly into the warmth before leaving again cannot fail to respond to these words. Although this passage is often quoted as a Christian view of the world, in fact, the speaker had not yet converted. It seems likely therefore that it was a *heathen* perception of life and the afterlife.

Another possibility of course is that Bede made up the speech, a practice that was quite common in early histories. Perhaps Bede intended to highlight the inability of the heathen faith to answer the 'deep questions'(Davidson 1973:222). Yet the fact that so many heathens reverted to their old faith after conversion suggests that Christianity did not always answer the 'deep questions' either. Possibly the mass conversions described by Bede were politically motivated rather than an expression of new-found religious faith.

Although the nature of the idols and statues in Coifi's temple is not very clear, there is some other evidence for them. In Ælfric's 'Lives of the Saints' they are described as being made by blacksmiths, describing how they would one day hammer the 'half made god' or carve out its eye 'with a stylus' – suggestive of Woden - but that as soon as the statue was finished would worship it. Figures of iron could have been smashed or melted down after the Conversion.

Also it's worth remembering that blacksmiths were often regarded as potent magicians all over Europe and were protected by their own blacksmithing deities such as the Greek Hephaistos, the Roman Vulcan and the Anglo-Saxon Wayland.   So iron statues would have been regarded as magically powerful especially once they had been consecrated. Ælfric's comments show an awareness that until consecration they remained merely an object. Once consecrated however they were empowered with the spirit or energy of the divine.

Ælfric also describes images as being made in 'various materials.' These might have been bone or wood, which either did not survive or has not yet been discovered. However, it is important to remember that by Ælfric's time, some heathen images would have been Viking and not Anglo-Saxon.

Going back in time a little further, Gildas (c.504-570) mentions 'those diabolical idols of my country' although does not name them (Works II.4). He does however state that, '...we still see some mouldering away within or without the deserted temples, with stiff and deformed features as was customary'.

The use of the word 'mouldering' rather than rusting or crumbling suggests figures made of wood or other organic material. Although Gildas does not say whether the figures represented humans or animals, their 'stiff and deformed features' suggests they were meant to depict something recognisable rather than just abstract patterns. Boniface also remarked that heathen gods were made of 'corruptible matter....[in] the likeness of a body.' (Bede EHEN II: 10). This implies that statues resembled humans (and possibly even animals) and were probably made of wood rather than stone.

Nevertheless Gildas' account remains at odds with Bede, who records that Eorcenberht of Kent was the first of to give orders for the complete abandonment and destruction of idols throughout his realm (EHEN III:8) This occurred c. 640 CE, almost a century after Gildas described them as already abandoned and rotting.

Perhaps different parts of England were more thorough in how they destroyed the statues, or perhaps they were indeed retained and kept in use much longer than the Church would have cared to admit.

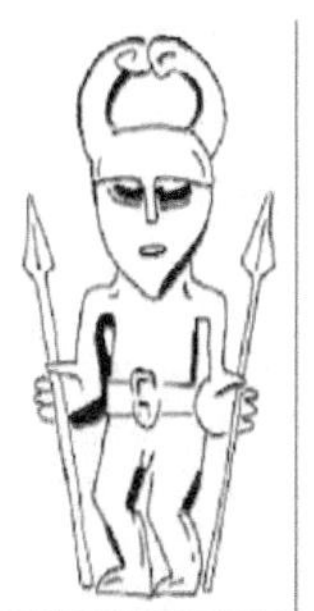

Chapter Eight

Women, Children and Family

A

lthough the early Christian Penitentials were noticeably anti-women, Christian missionaries seem to have specifically targeted the Christian wives of heathen Anglo-Saxon leaders to help them in their conversion work. Such wives were encouraged, nagged and even bribed to persuade their husbands to convert to Christianity.

For example, in 625 BCE, Pope Boniface wrote to Edwin, King of Northumbria, begging him to 'abhor idols and their worship... and the follies of temples and the deceitful flatteries of auguries.' (Bede EHEN II:10). When his appeal fell on deaf ears, Pope Boniface changed tack and wrote instead to King Edwin's Consort, Ethelberga, warning her to 'refrain from the worship of idols, and the deceits of temples and auguries.' He also sent valuable gifts including '...a silver looking-glass, and a gilt ivory comb,' to King Edwin of Northumbria's wife (Bede EHEN: II:11).

This exchange tells us a great deal about Church tactics and politics. It is not just that heathens had temples, idols and practised augury although this is an interesting insight. However, once a King converted he had to obey the Church in almost all things since religious influence went hand in hand with political and military power. In Anglo-Saxon times, converting the English people was a bit like playing chess – capture the King and the game was won.

Yet although missionaries made use of Christian wives to convert their husbands, while pouncing on the smallest deviation from Christian orthodoxy in other women, the Christian clergy at that time were not forced to be celibate. In Northern Europe at least, many were married (Burchard Paragraph 78A). These married clergy seem to have been particularly unpopular, and people often refused to attend mass or confession if they were officiating. The situation got so bad in some parts of Christendom that the Church had to threaten people with penance if they persisted in avoiding them!

Amongst the laity, some heathen Anglo-Saxons continued to have several wives and concubines even *after* they were converted. This had potentially far reaching implications as far as the Church was concerned since a concubine's children could inherit from their father if he wished. Naturally the Church taught that having concubines was illegal and immoral, declaring all offspring of such unions to be illegitimate. This represented a major change in that now such children could no longer inherit even if the father wished to leave them property.

This meant the Church would then acquire the property of a man who died without legitimate heirs. As a result, not only individuals but also even tribes could lose control over their own property (Ross 1985:6). Yet drastic though this sounds, it probably did not concern the majority of ordinary people, who owned very little and were liable to be enslaved at any time.

The lives of women in Anglo-Saxon society varied according to age, marital status, wealth, etc. They would also have been affected by periods of warfare, since their status was liable to change dramatically if their husbands or fathers were killed or they and their children were enslaved. This was not unique to the pre-Conversion period either, for strife and warfare of one kind or another persisted right up to the Norman Invasion of 1066 and beyond.

Higher class women often endured double standards. Although more free than their later Norman counterparts, they were frequently segregated from men outside the family and sometimes – after the Conversion – sent to live in convents. Yet outwardly the Anglo-Saxons seem to have been quite liberal in their outlook towards marriage even in the post Conversion period. In the laws of Cnut (11.74) we are told, '...and neither a widow nor a maiden is ever to be forced to marry a man whom she herself dislikes, nor to be given for money, unless he chooses to give anything of his own free will.' (quoted in Ross 1985:8) In fairness however, we cannot be sure whether such lofty ideals were always observed or enforced in practice.

Given the early Church's restrictive views on sex and marriage, it was remarkable the human race survived. For example, Pope Gregory informed Augustine that a man who had recently had sex should not enter a church, '...for the desire itself can by no means be without sin' (Bede EHEN Book I: 27)

Some of the most intriguing evidence for the status of Anglo-Saxon children comes from the early Christian Church's acceptance of child monks and nuns, known as oblates. This was not confined to Anglo Saxon England but was common all over Europe from the sixth century onwards (Herlihy 1978:

118).

Indeed, Bede wrote of his own childhood, 'I was born on the lands of this monastery, and on reaching seven years of age I was entrusted by my family first to the most reverent Abbot Benedict and later to Abbot Ceofrid for my education.'(Bede EHEN V:24) Bede never again left the monastery, so almost everything he knew of the secular world pre-dated his eighth birthday.

In the seventh century, for example, St Wilfrid had stated that a boy of seven was the right age to become a monk and this age may well be significant both for Christians and heathens. Heathen burials suggest there may have been some rite of passage for boys at around this age because the grave goods undergo significant changes.

This poses several questions: What happened to those children who remained in their own families and communities? Did the boys start to train in the arts of fighting? Or did they begin learning the oral poetry and religious traditions of their own family and community? We simply cannot answer unless or until more evidence comes to light.

Asser, who wrote a biography of King Alfred much later in the Anglo Saxon period (the ninth century, although some believe it could have been even later) complained that children were sometimes the only voluntary candidates for monastic orders. He believed this was because they had not yet grown used to the materialistic pursuits of adults (Kuefler 1991:825).

Possibly at around the age of seven, heathen children were sent away to be fostered with other families. This is supported in Beowulf, where we read, 'I was seven winters old when the lord of treasures, the gracious ruler of peoples, received me from my father' (cited in Brentano 1964:246). By the Middle Ages, the elite regularly sent their children to be fostered with other families of similar status.

However, when a child from a wealthy family took holy orders, his inheritance eventually passed to the church. A child who was fostered in another household however, was more likely to marry and have heirs of his/her own. Therefore the Church may have opposed such arrangements because it denied them new candidates for the monasteries. Newly converted families may not have found it difficult to send their children to monasteries and convents because they would have sent their children away to other families at that age anyway.

Similar concerns may have been behind the early Church's disapproval of hiring wet nurses. At the time (and for centuries thereafter) it was believed breast feeding prevented conception. A mother who handed her child over to a wet nurse therefore was considered more likely to fall pregnant again. More children meant more heirs and less likelihood that the line would die out and the estate could eventually pass to the Church as vacant land (Goody 1983 :40).

The Church took this 'problem' so seriously in the late sixth century that Pope Gregory the Great wrote about it to Augustine of Canterbury. Yet the practice continued into the late seventh/early eighth century and even King Alfred's children had wet nurses. The fact that the Church was so flagrantly disobeyed suggests people were not fooled; and resisted the Church's efforts to claim ever more land and wealth, especially from those who died without heirs.

There are other curious patterns in the distribution of grave goods in child graves. For example, children over the age of three were sometimes buried with a knife, while very young children were either buried with a pot or even no goods at all. Perhaps this suggests either that they were not regarded as 'real' people at that age, or did not need anything to offer when they reached the afterlife Perhaps their young age assured them of successful entry.

Spears were often buried with boys aged between ten and fourteen, although sometimes they turn up with younger boys of around seven as do arrow heads. Perhaps spear throwing or archery were the first military and hunting skills that boys learned, and perhaps a year or so later, around the age of ten or eleven they began taking part in the male orientated activities of the family and community.

Of course this in turn poses the question – did the family or community mark a boy's acquiring a spear or bow by any rite of passage? All over the world, many cultures do mark the entrance of a boy into manhood at around the age of twelve. Possibly the Anglo-Saxons also held some sort of ceremony that accompanied the gift or use of his first weapons. We cannot say for certain, but presumably the weapons would have been the subject of spells to ensure they protected the young bearer.

Likewise female identity seems to undergo changes at certain ages. Infant girls were often buried with beads, but after the age of five their jewellery included disc brooches suggesting this had become a symbol of her change in status (Stoodley 2000:462).

Going on the evidence of grave goods, girls seem to have reached a second threshold at around the age of twelve. From the evidence of grave goods, girls of twelve were now entitled to wear two more elaborate disc brooches, one on each shoulder, usually with strings of beads between them. Sometimes these were decorated with cruciforms or swastikas. They also began wearing rings. From around the age of fifteen, girls began wearing two much heavier saucer or square headed brooches together with girdle ornaments and keys.

It is of course tempting to assume that this was the age when they reached puberty and began menstruating, and that the changes in status signified their ability to bear children. However, we cannot be sure when girls reached puberty in the sixth and seventh centuries. Even in the early twentieth century many girls did not reach puberty until around the age of fifteen.

Possibly girls did have three distinct landmarks in their status, the first at age five, then twelve and fifteen. Boys may have had just two, one at around seven, and another between ten and twelve. It is also possible that different age landmarks varied from one kingdom to another.

Although there is so much we do not know, we can still surmise that – for both sexes – these thresholds were marked by certain weapons or dress ornaments perhaps given as gifts. Also in many societies, these rites-of-passage are often linked to religious and magical ceremonies that involve the whole family or community.   There is no reason to suppose that the Anglo-Saxons would have done things differently.

Chapter Nine

Changing the gods to mortals and devils

I

n converting the Anglo-Saxons, the Church had to get rid of the heathen deities. Unfortunately there are no heathen texts to tell us about them; everything we have is from a Christian point of view such as Ælfric's homily, 'On the False Gods.' This – somewhat unwittingly – reveals a little of heathen practices in England. Ælfric (c. 955 – c. 1010) was a Christian Abbot although his name is curiously heathen, meaning 'elf ruler.' It was an ironic name for someone so intent on wiping out all memory of heathen beliefs and customs.

The easiest method of erasing heathen deities was to assimilate them into Christian saints with similar characteristics. This syncretising – equating gods from different traditions – is not unique to Christianity. It was also popular among the pagan Romans who appropriated deities from newly captured provinces and then morphed them with their own.

However assimilation could only succeed if the people were reasonably amenable and if the gods in question were suitable. Deities such as Baldur and Frey were relatively easy to assimilate. The Anglo-Saxon poem, 'Dream of the Rood' shows Baldur as a Christ-like figure, a bleeding god on a tree.

The name Frey was not only given to the god, but was also a common metaphor for a secular lord. It was sometimes applied to Anglo-Saxon Kings and even to describe the Christian God (Chaney 1970 :51). Frey was also sometimes known as Ing, perhaps derived from Yngvi-Frey, a god of peace and plenty who was relatively easily absorbed within Christianity.

Of course, if people resisted such assimilation or if the god proved impossible to Christianise, then the Church resorted to demonization, by equating the heathen god with the Christian devil. For example, an old Saxon Baptismal vow from c. 8th century states, ' I renounce all the words and works of the devil, Thunaer, Woden and Saxnot, and all those demons who are their companions' (quoted in Turville-Petre 1964:100).

However, this too presented problems. Woden was not just a god, he was a political force. Virtually every Anglo-Saxon kingdom claimed descent from him, with only the East Saxons claiming descent from Seax-neat, (who was also known to the European Saxons). Woden and his traditions proved very difficult to eradicate until the majority of kingdoms had converted to Christianity. In the Exeter Book's *Maxims*, we read, 'Woden made idols, the Almighty [made] glory, the spacious heavens.' This seems a deliberate attempt to enhance the Christian God by downplaying Woden's role as a Sky-Father deity.

Ælfric is a useful source for learning about heathen practices. For example, he tells us how people worshipped 'the sun and moon as gods because of their shining brightness, and they made offerings to them.' He also describes the importance of the elements, 'Some ...believed in fire because of its rapid burning, some also in water, and they worshipped them as gods; some in the earth because it feeds all things' (Ælfric, On the False Gods, 1967-8). Another possibility is that fire refers to Thunor and earth to Frig.

In daily life however, the heathen deities were ever present. We still constantly use the names of the Anglo-Saxon gods whenever we mention the days of the week: Tiw (Tuesday); Woden (Wednesday), Thunor (Thursday) and Frig or Fricg (Friday) the Anglo-Saxon equivalent of Odin's wife Freya.

Ælfric also tries to explain some divine attributes. For example, '[Thunor's] ...son is called Mars, and he was forever creating conflict, and he would always stir up contention and woe'. Although using the Latin name, Mars, Ælfric was referring to Tiw, god of battle, who was 'worshipped... as a lofty god, and whenever they campaigned or would go to battle, first they would make offerings to this god.'

Although Ælfric does not explain exactly what offerings were made or how, he does show an underlying principle of reciprocity, i.e. that offerings were made in order to obtain a desired result. If his claim is true, then it shows us something of the Anglo-Saxons' relationship with Tiw. Archaeologists have

discovered many weapons marked with the Tiw Rune **ᛏ** which must have been intended to protect the bearer and make him successful in battle.

Ælfric makes no attempt to disguise how much he hated Woden. Even Jove (Jupiter/Zeus) and Thunor were described as the most 'venerable of all the gods.' Yet of Woden he writes, '...he was very dishonest and deceitful in his deeds, and also loved stealing and falsehood' (On the False Gods, 1967-8).

Despite his loathing, Ælfric unwittingly provides a few clues about rituals associated with Woden, with people bringing 'offerings to him at crossroads and... sacrifices to him on high mountains.'

Possibly the Church regarded Woden as dangerous because of his association with all things wild. The medieval German chronicler, Adam of Bremen claimed 'Wodan, id est furor' meaning 'Woden, that is to say, Fury' (Ryan, 1963: 474). The Old English *wodendream* is often equated with the Latin *furor animi*, a type of delirious madness.

Certainly from an early date, Woden had established himself as the most important of the Anglo-Saxon gods. Even heroes such as Hengist and Horsa claimed descent from him *via* Godwulf of Geat. Nennius, in his eighth century *Historia Brittorum* does not actually name Woden, but cannot be referring to anyone else, when he writes of, '...one of their idols... blinded by some demon' (Nennius, III:31)

The Church was determined to weaken Woden's influence. One method was to change place names connected with him (such as barrows and burial mounds) so that they now incorporated 'Devil' or 'Adam' in their name. For example, Wansdyke, (almost certainly built long before the Saxons arrived) become known as the Devil's Ditch after the Conversion. It was rumoured to have been built by the Devil on a Wednesday, which was of course, Woden's day

Before long, Wednesday became regarded as an unlucky day, although like Thursday, it was also considered a good day for sowing and planting crops (Chaney 1970:35). Possibly in heathen times, Wednesday had been considered lucky, and then, like everything else connected with Woden, this meaning was turned on its head.

Gods were also demoted by changing them into giants, hence the many legends about giants (originally pre-Christian gods) that became associated with ancient burial mounds and sacred sites. Clearly it proved extremely difficult to eradicate heathen deities completely from popular consciousness.

Woden is well attested in northern Europe from quite early times and his name may originally have been Wodanz deriving from an early word meaning wind, breath, and spirit. If true, then perhaps his original function was as a sky or storm god. This could then be linked to his role as one of the original leaders of the Wild Hunt.

There are folk traditions in many countries that tell of a Wild Hunt led by a supernatural huntsman who gathers up souls. Witnesses who included some monks, heard them shouting and winding their horns. The account appears in the Peterborough Chronicle for the year 1127 CE, and although Woden is not mentioned by name, he could easily be the Wild Huntsman in his cloak and wide brimmed bat. As late as the early twelfth century, people reported seeing the hunt in a deer park at Peterborough and as far afield as Stamford.

Some of the less well known divine figures are particularly interesting. For instance, it is difficult to be certain whether the magical blacksmith Wayland (sometimes written as Weland) was worshipped as a god or revered as a hero. He was certainly well known in England and northern Europe and his name probably derived from the proto-Germanic verb *welan* meaning 'to work dexterously, with craft' (Bradley 1990:41).

Wayland must have been important because several places were named after him. Wayland's Smithy, for example is a megalithic stone grave, situated on the Ridgeway, not far from the Berkshire White Horse. According to a Berkshire charter of 855 CE, (a time when all the heathen deities should have been long since forgotten) it was still being referred to as *Waylands smiðða* or Wayland's Smithy (Davidson 1963: 531).

According to tradition, any traveller whose horse lost a shoe, should leave the horse at the 'smithy' along with some money. When he returned the money would be gone and the horse would be shod. Such beliefs persisted right into the twentieth century. Not so long ago I heard it claimed that Wayland has moved into the age of the motor car and now repairs punctures too!

According to tradition, Wayland was the son of the storm giant Wade, who built castles and Roman roads in various places including Yorkshire. Giants – as we have seen – were often once gods, and it is possible that Wade was an Anglo-Saxon name for Woden. In many cultures, giants represented primordial deities, who were displaced (often by their own sons) and stripped of their power.

Wayland however, persisted into the post-Conversion period and even makes several appearances in literature. There is a brief reference to 'the ancient smith' Wayland in Beowulf, (Beowulf 405-6, 454-55) who made the hero's armour. Although the earliest Beowulf manuscript dates c.1000 CE, the story itself is very much earlier.

Wayland is also mentioned in the early Anglo-Saxon poem, *Deor's Lament*, in the Exeter Book, where Deor comforts himself by thinking of Wayland's hardships when he was put in fetters by King Nibhad, and of Beahohild's sorrow when she discovered Wayland had made her pregnant. The *Lament*, dating c. late tenth century, suggests Wayland's story was already very old. It also reveals a fascinating glimpse into the nature of the Anglo-Saxon character. After listing so many dreadful events, the refrain adds hopefully, ' þ aes ofereode, þ isses swa mæg!' (That passed away, so may this!')

King Alfred the Great's late ninth century translation of Boethius's *De consolation philosophiae* (Book 2 Chapter 7) also mentions Wayland. Curiously, the author changed the original text, 'Where are now the bones of staunch Fabricius?' (a Roman general) to 'What now are Wayland, the famous and wise goldsmith's bones?'

One of the earliest artefacts to visually depict Wayland is the Franks' Casket, a small whalebone box covered with narrative scenes and inscribed with runes. This may date from as early as c.700 CE (Northumbria) or as late as c.950 CE (Yorkshire) (Vandersall, 1972: 23).

The front panel of the casket tells the story using the technique of continuous narrative, i.e. combining several scenes even though they happened at different times. This was most effective when viewers already knew the story of how Wayland had been captured by King Nithhad and cruelly hamstrung. Although forced to work for the king, the smith plotted his revenge. He killed one of the king's sons and made a golden cup from his head which he then offered to Beahohild, the king's daughter, who had brought a magic ring for Wayland to repair.

On the left we see Wayland surrounded by his anvil, hammer and a lifeless body, together with Wayland offering Beahohild the cup made from her brother's skull. This contains the drugged potion that enabled Wayland to rape her. The third figure on the right is variously interpreted as a servant carrying a flask or the pregnant and deserted Beahohild after Wayland's escape. The right hand side of the panel shows a man with birds, usually identified as Wayland's brother, Egill. Egill killed birds to make a set of wings to enable Wayland to fly away and escape. Even nowadays it is difficult to remain unmoved by the effortless blend of magic and horror in Wayland's story.

Although Loki is well known in Scandinavian mythology, it is difficult to find his equivalent among the Anglo-Saxons. Such representations that do exist probably date from after the Viking invasions. Until c.1890 it was believed that Loki was virtually unknown in England. Then a clergyman wrote a letter to the author and folklorist Baring-Gould, describing an incident from his Lincolnshire childhood, back in 1859.

According to the letter, his mother had sent him with some quinine to visit a local 'wise woman' whose grandson was ill. Although she accepted the first bottle of quinine, when the boy was sent to take her a second bottle she refused, claiming that she knew a better cure than 'yon mucky stuff.'

She then showed the young boy her grandson's bed, where three horseshoes had been nailed to the wooden footboard with a hammer laid across them. She explained that she used to take the hammer in her left hand and strike the shoes three times, while saying:

Feyther, Son an' Holi Ghoast,

Naale the divil to this poast.

Throice I stroikes with holy crook,

Won for God, an' won for Wod, an' won for Lok.

The woman then explained that this charm ensured that 'Whin the Old Un comes to shak him he wean't nivver git past you; you'ull fin' him saafe as t' church steaple' (Baring Gould 1913:77).

Nor was that the end of the matter. Eight years after the original account, the same vicar had another account published by the Folklore Society (Folklore, 9, 1898: 186). The author now claimed that the old woman had actually demonstrated to him how it was done. And four years after *that*, in 1902, the vicar lectured to the Viking Society, adding an extra line so that the charm now read:

Feyther, Son an' Holi Ghoast,

Naale the divil to this poast.

Throice I smoites with Holy Crok,

With this mell Oi throice dew knock,

One for God, An' one for Wod, An' one for Lok (Davidson 1963: 535)

Although the vicar's mother had apparently suggested that Wod meant Woden while Lok meant Loki, another interpretation is that striking the horseshoe with a hammer was meant to represent a third deity, Thunor.

It is a fascinating story, the sort we would really *like* to believe. Perhaps the vicar's tale was indeed the last remnant of a popular tradition once widely practised, but later lost. Or maybe it was little more than wishful thinking, embellished and ornamented to prove a point.

Unfortunately no other supporting evidence followed, and no other country folk came forward with their hammers and horseshoes for 'nailing' a fever. But before dismissing the tale completely, it is worth remembering there are many similar folk remedies, such as Nail Trees, where illnesses were quite literally nailed to a tree. And many Nail Trees were oaks, which were traditionally associated with the god Thunor.

It is also true there are similarities between the footboard striking ritual and some Anglo-Saxon charms, 'If a man's head be distorted, lay the man with face upward; drive two stakes into the ground at the armpits, then place a plank obliquely over the feet and strike three times upon it with a sledge-hammer. His skull will soon be right' (Grendon 1909:137). Magically this is based on like curing like, with the blows to the plank representing blows to the injured head.

A century ago, historians and antiquaries would eagerly jump to conclusions. Nowadays it is just as fashionable to brush everything aside as unproven. The truth probably lies somewhere In-between.

Chapter Ten

Horses and Priests

S

ometimes, even though the evidence is scarce, it seems likely that certain Anglo-Saxon magical and religious beliefs did exist, if we are not sure exactly what they were called. It seems probable, for example, that there was an Anglo-Saxon cult of the horse exemplified by several large white horses that were cut into the turf in southern England. Whether this was something the Anglo-Saxons brought with them, or something they found when they arrived and then adopted, we cannot be certain. The famous White Horse of Oxfordshire for example, was once thought to have been made by King Alfred although it is now believed to be much older.

Other Anglo-Saxon sites nearby, such as the Ridgeway and Wayland's Smithy suggest that the Anglo-Saxons were drawn to an area previously regarded as sacred.   If the White Horse pre-dates the Anglo-Saxons, then its preservation indicates that it was not incompatible with their own beliefs and traditions. We cannot help but be reminded of Tacitus' description of the pure white horses used for divination (Germania 10.68). Their neighs and whinnies were interpreted by a priest acting as their servant, while 'the horses are the confidants of the gods.'

Later in the same work Tacitus describes how the Tencteri tribe handed down horses '...as part of the household with its protecting gods and the rights of succession' (*Germania*: 32). This suggests a more private religious ritual, where horses, household gods and even the rights of inheritance are all inextricably intertwined. We also know that horses were important in later Scandinavian traditions about magical steeds such as Hrimfaxi and Skinfaxi.

However virtually nothing similar has survived in the Anglo-Saxon records apart from the story of the twin brothers, Hengist (stallion) and Horsa (horse). Their names appear in places such as Horsington (in Somerset and Lincolnshire), Hinksey (Berkshire) and Henstridge (Somerset).

According to legend, Hengist and Horsa arrived in England as part of the earliest Anglo-Saxon invasions, and at the request of the British King Vortigern who was fighting off Pictish invasions. Ultimately the alliance turned sour, Vortigern was ousted, while Hengist became king of Kent after his brother Horsa was killed in battle against the British.

Looking at a slightly wider picture, we see that the story has curious similarities with that of Rome's twin founders, Romulus and Remus. In both instances, one brother dies violently while the other eventually becomes the leader of a great nation.

Also Tacitus may provide some useful clues, with his description of how a Germanic tribe called the Naharvali worshipped two brother gods called the Alci. In turn, the Alci are often equated with the classical twins, Castor and Pollux (Germania: 44) known collectively as the Dioscuri. Like Hengist and Horsa they were closely associated with horses and according to Tacitus their rituals took place in a hallowed grove.

Tacitus also described how the Naharvali's presiding priest '...dresses like a woman' (Germania: 43). This is very interesting, because it seems the Anglo-Saxons had something similar. In Grave Nine at Portway in Hampshire, archaeologists discovered a male body, aged about fifty, buried with female jewellery (Wilson 1992: 96). Although the grave clothes had rotted away, it is quite possible that these too, were women's attire. Hall (2007:154) believes that some 'cross-dressing' men may have been ritual specialists.

The same burial also revealed carbonised grained of wheat which again provides a link with northern Europe. Burning grain where a corpse has rested was expressly prohibited by the early Church. So despite the fact that both Tacitus and authors such as Burchard were writing about continental Germanic tribes, and that neither were specifically concerned with the Anglo-Saxons, there is some supporting evidence in Anglo-Saxon archaeology that *some* practices made their way to England.

Another interesting feature of the same Portway burial was the presence of a large flint on its chest. Traditionally this was sometimes done in order to prevent the dead from 'walking'. Alternatively - since the Anglo-Saxons believed that flints were made by elves - the dead man may have been some sort of shaman or performed magical work that connected various worlds, or even that he worked with elves.

Unfortunately most of what we know about Anglo-Saxon priests was written by Christian clergy, who describe them only in terms of their eventual conversion. A burial at Yeavering in Northumbria however is thought to be that of a priest. It lies on an east/west alignment, the head facing west and a goat's skull buried at its feet.

The grave also contained curious three staff-like objects, suggesting some sort of ritual status. The first staff was a long wooden shaft with bronze bindings and an iron spike at the top. Fixed to the base, positioned near the goat's skull was an animal effigy that has been identified variously as a sheep, goat or even a crested bird. The second, much shorter, staff lay near the feet at a right angle to the first and had bronze terminals. The third staff lay underneath the longest staff, and extended from the body's left shoulder to its right hip where it terminated in an iron spike. (Wilson 1992: 176)

What can this tell us? Perhaps there was a cult of the goat. To support the idea, we see that the Anglo Saxon *bucc* and *bucca* (goat and he-goat respectively) turn up in place names such as Bucklesham, Buckworth, Buckingham and Bucknall (Mawer 1919:236). Although fascinating, it is hardly conclusive evidence. It certainly cannot tell us what such priests may have done, how they dressed, acted or spoke, or how they were regarded in their society.

This is where we must turn again to authors such as Tacitus, who wrote about the continental ancestors of the man buried at Yeavering. He tells us many things – such as priests casting lots or interpreting the neighing of horses as auspices (Germania: 10).   Unfortunately, Tacitus mostly gives only the classical equivalents for the Germanic gods worshipped in groves. His account of how the Anglii tribe worshipped 'Nerthus, or Mother Earth,' raises interesting possibilities however (Germania : 40). It is possible – though not entirely provable – that this is the 'Erce, Mother of Earth' who is invoked in one of the Anglo-Saxon Charms.

According to Tacitus the Anglii believed that Nerthus 'interests herself in human affairs and rides through their peoples.' He then goes on to specifically mention Britain, the, '...Island of Ocean...[where] stands a sacred grove, and in the grove stands a car [chariot] draped with a cloth which none but the priest may touch.' Festivities accompany the goddess as she is taken in her chariot around her lands, 'No one goes to war, no one takes up arms; every object of iron is locked away; and then and then only, are peace and quiet known and prized.'

At last, the goddess returns to her temple with her priest, and then specially chosen slaves washed down the goddess (suggesting a statue, although it may have been a human representative) together with her chariot. Finally the unfortunate slaves were drowned to prevent them telling what they had seen. This hints that the cult of Nerthus could have been some type of mystery religion.

Of course, Tacitus was describing a British ritual practised by a continental Germanic tribe during a time of Roman occupation. We simply do not know whether the ritual originated with the pre-Roman Celtic people or whether it was imported into England by a Germanic tribe and then re-introduced perhaps with the arrival of the Anglo-Saxons in the fifth century. However it remains a very intriguing glimpse into the practices of ancient peoples in northern Europe.

Chapter Eleven

How and what they celebrated

One thing that regularly comes across about the Anglo-Saxons and their northern ancestors is their love of celebration. Indeed, they seem to have regarded heaven as one unending feast (Chaney 1970:68). Ultimately the Church Christianised many of their festivals such as Yule and Eostre. The Anglo-Saxons' joy in celebration however has not been lost and many of the traditions we take for granted nowadays probably owe a great deal to them.

It is sometimes claimed the Anglo-Saxons recognised only two seasons, summer and winter. However they may have recognised four: spring (*Ver*), summer (*Aestas*), autumn (*Autumnus*) and winter (*Hiems*). Their dates were as follows although we cannot be sure whether these were traditional names or the creation of later Christian writers (Lapidge *et al* 2007:231):

- 7th February - beginning of Spring.
- 9th May – beginning of Summer.
- 7th August – beginning of Autumn.
- 7th November – beginning of Winter. (Tupper 1895:203)

Much of what we know about the Anglo-Saxon months of the year comes from Bede, and in this respect not everyone agrees that he is entirely reliable. For example, he states that the year was calculated by the moon, which would give thirteen, not twelve months. Yet he also claims the year was divided into ten, with two months, Giuli and Litha being of double length. The resulting calendar was:

January	Giuli or *æftera-geola* meaning 'after Yule'
February	Solmonath
March	Hrethmonath
April	Eosturmonath
May	Thrimilchi
June	Litha
July	also called Litha (a double month)
August	Wodmonath
September	Halegmonath
October	Winterfilleth
November	Blodmonath
December	Giuli (a double month with January) or Yule

The importance of the Midwinter and Midsummer solstices (celebrated on December 25th and June 24th respectively) may explain why they fall in 'double' months.

According to the Anglo Saxon Chronicle, midwinter celebrations could last between twelve and twenty days (Tupper 1895:204). The Equinoxes were usually placed at March 25th and September 24th.

The date of New Year varied in Anglo-Saxon times and could include December 24th. The Anglo-Saxon Chronicle only describes January 1st as New Year once in 1096 (some thirty years after the Battle of Hastings.) Yet in 673 CE, Theodore of Canterbury's Penitential set out harsh penalties for anyone celebrating this day. We do not know exactly how they celebrated, but across Northern Europe people dressed up as animals, usually stags or calves. (much to the annoyance, presumably, of the Church authorities).

According to Bede's *De Temporum Ratione* (The Reckoning of Time), February was called Solmonath because it was 'the month of the cakes which, in it, they used to offer to their gods.' It has been suggested that during this month the Anglo Saxons baked cakes in the shapes of birds and animals as symbols of their gods (Owen 1981:49). However the OE *sol* may also mean 'mire,' and even in recent times February was nicknamed 'February Fill-Dyke' in reference to the heavy rains that are common at this time of year.

Bede is the only source who suggests Hrethmonath (March) was named after the goddess Hretha. We know virtually nothing about this goddess, although *Retmonat* and *Redimonat* do appear in German sources while Rheda (or Hreda) may derive from the Old English *hred* meaning fame and honour. Other possibilities are that the name simply meant a fierce or swift month or even that Hrethe was an Anglo-Saxon version of the goddess Nerthus who is mentioned in Tacitus' *Germania* (40.133-34)

Likewise Bede is our only source of information for Eosturmonath which he claims was named after the heathen goddess Eostre 'in whose honour feasts were celebrated in that month. Now they designate the Paschal season by her name, calling the joys of the new rite by the time-honoured name of the old observance' (Bede in Wallis 1999:54).

From this it is clear how some aspects of heathenism persisted and were assimilated into the Christian festivals and calendar. Modern scholars however are less convinced. Some suggest Eosturmonath meant the month of openings or beginnings (Hutton 1996:180). Yet even this interpretation may still tie in with Eostre as some sort of dawn goddess, (dawn being the beginning or opening of the new day.) Possibly Eostre was Bede's version of the Greek dawn goddess Eos.

Even if he intended to minimise heathenism and promote Christianity, inventing totally new deities seems a strange way to go about this. We have to find a balance between too much cynicism and finding evidence of paganism in every folk custom or nursery rhyme.

Basically, there is no harm in speculating provided we are honest about how much supporting evidence we can find. After all, myth is constantly changing even into modern times. It is therefore quite possible that Eostre was goddess of both the dawn and the spring equinox and that other knowledge of her has been lost or even misinterpreted. And since both Hrethmonath and Eosturmonath occur in spring, perhaps their rituals invoked fertility new growth.

Another possibility is that Eostre's festivities involved some sort of consecrated cake, later Christianised as the popular Easter Hot Cross Buns.

Heathen spring equinox festivities have proved remarkably resistant to change with Easter bunnies, hares, eggs and even pancakes honouring the moon all surviving into present times.

Bede claims the month of May was known as Thrimilchi because goats and cows could now be milked three times a day although he does not mention any specific deity associated with this month. The double month of Litha (June and July) signified mild weather, although *liđen* can also mean to travel or sail. Perhaps this reflects reluctance to attempt long sea journeys until the milder weather.

August was known as Weodmonath, meaning weed or grass month. Certainly both are plentiful at this time. It was also sometimes known as *Þridda-liđa*, the third mild month. On the first of August, celebrations known as *half-mæsse* or Lammas meaning a loaf mass or feast, was a time when offerings were made of bread from new corn. This festival could therefore be the original source of the harvest loaf shaped like a sheaf, which was often regarded a child of the grain deity (Chaney 1970:88).

The important of Lammas is shown by the fact that August 1st was Christianised early on, and Bede states 'it was agreed by all' that the Early Church should choose it for its annual Synod meetings at Clofeshoch, in the 670's CE. (EHEN IV: 5)

Although we do not know exactly how the heathen Anglo-Saxons celebrated Lammas, there are many traditions in England (and all over northern Europe) honouring the last stalk of corn or rye left in the field. This was almost always female, given nicknames such as Old Woman, Old Wife, The Mare, The Hag, or the Corn Maiden although sometimes the last sheaf was deliberately left for the 'Corn Man' as an offering to Woden.

September, or Halegmonath, meant a holy month or month of rituals. The Christian festival of Michaelmas (St Michael being a dragon slayer) is close to the Autumn Equinox which I have long suspected was considerably more important than most people now realise. Bede calls it 'the month of 'offerings' (*De Temporum Ratione* 13). The most likely recipient of these would probably have been Frey, god of fertility and plenty.

The name Winterfilleth for October emphasises its importance as the gateway to winter. According to Bede, November was known as Blotmonath or Blod-monath, meaning blood month, or month of sacrifice (*De Temporum Ratione* 15). The closest Christian equivalent to blot was communion, and the

Anglo Saxon word for communion, *husel or husul* is closely related to the Gothic *hunsl* which also means sacrifice. (Chaney 1970:69)

Although there is little evidence to suggest the Anglo-Saxons specifically honoured their dead during this month it is possible that the 'dying' of the year was magically linked to the dead and honouring ancestors. This is particularly likely given how closely the Anglo-Saxons lived with the natural world around them.

If we compare the November offerings, to those made in September, these sacrifices were of animals to the gods.   When winter feed was scarce, animals were, of necessity, slaughtered. This continued right up until the eighteenth century at around this time of year until reformed farming practices made it possible to feed more animals through the winter months. The Anglo-Saxons had no such choice, the animals had to be slaughtered and their meat smoked or salted to preserve it. Ever practical, they then dedicated the cull to their gods – most likely to Frey - in order to secure his support through the harsh winter months.

It is possible there was a special day (or days) set aside for this. The most likely date (bearing in mind that Pope Gregory advised selecting a saint's day close to a pagan festival) is somewhere around 11th November. This is not only close to the old heathen Winter's Day festival on the 7th November, (when the king made sacrifices to ensure a good year ahead) but was later Christianised as St Martin's Day (Martinmas).

Yuletide celebrations lasted for twelve nights and thirteen days, which perhaps explains why it was one of the two double months of the year, the extra time being needed to accommodate it. Celebrations began with the first new or the first full moon after the winter solstice.

The origins of the word 'Yule' are sometimes disputed. It may derive from *Geol*, where *ol* means 'ale'(Tupper 1895:205), showing the season's close association with feasting. However the name could derive from *Gehweol*, a wheel. Although it has long been traditional to roll a blazing, straw covered wheel downhill at the midsummer solstice, a similar tradition does not seem to have survived for midwinter. Certainly a blazing straw wheel would be very effective on a cold dark winter's night and it is possible that such a tradition did exist during the pre-Conversion period.

Yule was magically associated with good fortune, since three 'lucky birthdays' occurred on consecutive days (December 31st – January 2nd) during this period (Chaney 1970:60). The number three recurs often in the Anglo-Saxon Charms. Some Yuletide traditions, especially divination for love or weather, persisted well into the nineteenth century. In any rural community, knowing what the weather would be like in the coming year was vital, and suggests a strong element of fertility magic was also involved.

North European fertility festivals seem to have been very physical, involving jumping off tables, leaping over midsummer fires, dancing, rolling and ringing bells – enough to make anyone giddy. In fact 'giddy' comes from the Anglo-Saxon *gydig* which meant to engage with a god (Hall 2007:149). The Christian penitentials often complained about dancing, so perhaps spinning and even circle dancing were common factors in heathen Anglo-Saxon religious and magical ritual. Feeling giddy afterwards could have been regarded as a sign that the ritual had been successful.

Straw was also associated with Yule in traditions that may date back to Anglo-Saxon times. In Germany people wrapped bands of straw for protection around trees during Yule and on New Year's Eve, while in England there was an old tradition that to see a pig with straw in its mouth first thing in the morning it foretold marriage and many children. The god Frey was associated with fertility and boars, and people made offerings to him, Woden and Holda, right across northern Europe.

Originally these offerings included pease, beans and meal, but eventually bread made in various shapes became popular and possibly even replaced earlier animal sacrifices (De Cleene 2003 Vol 2:105). One example could be the Scandinavian Yule Horse Bread, made in the shape of a horse or plaited loaves to symbolise human hair. The original meanings of the various spirals, double spirals, circles and loops used in bread-making however are long forgotten. We can now only guess at what they might have represented.

Other offerings could have included specially baked round cakes representing the sun or moon, or marked into segments in honour of the sun wheel or even the seasons. Some breads and cakes were particularly popular around Christmas time, and many are still made. Bread and cakes were – and still are - considered appropriate offerings for many festivals and not just Yule! For example they can mark important rites of passage such as births, funerals and weddings.

The wheat cult was particularly associated with Holda, who appears in several guises as 'Old Gal' or 'Old Woman' in English folk tradition. She may also have been associated with geese, especially in wintertime. When it snowed in Victorian England, country children still described it as 'The Old Woman is plucking her geese' while in Europe it was 'Frau Holle is shaking her featherbed.'

According to Bede, Christmas Eve was for a long time known as Modraniht which literally means the night of the mothers.' (*De Temporum Ratione* quoted in Wallis 1999:53). Exactly who these mothers were is open to debate. Groups of three female deities were popular in Celtic, Germanic, and Norse culture. However Bede does not mention how many there were, although even if they were sisters, there is no reason they could not also have been mothers. so perhaps they even represented the Wyrd Sisters. It has also been suggested that Modraniht refers to the Sun as a female divinity (in most cultures the Sun tends to be masculinised) (Turner 1836:I.233). Alternatively, the 'mothers' could have been real people who held some sort of nocturnal vigil on Christmas Eve.

One problem with the early Christian writers is their tendency to synchronise deities, e.g. equating Frig with Venus and Aphrodite. This is something they probably inherited from the Roman *interpretatio romana* and can be very confusing. Certainly as late as the end of the tenth century, Bishop Burchard of Worms rebuked women for laying three places at the table for the Parcae (whose name means 'to bring forth.) Although he uses the Roman term, Burchard was born and ministered his entire life within what we now call Germany. It seems very likely therefore that he *was* preaching against local, Germanic traditions, even if he gave them a Roman name. Of course this does not prove that the same traditions were being practised by Anglo Saxons in England, although it is quite possible especially in view of Bede's statements about a night of the mothers.

A quick glance at some north European traditions concerning cakes provides some more clues about the celebratory use of cakes etc. It is certainly possibly the Anglo-Saxons took many traditions with them when they left their European homelands.

In Germany, for example, jam or custard doughnuts were supposed to be a relic of baked arrowheads offered to the earth goddess during February (Peters 1918: 100). Arrowheads also resemble hearts and may have continued in this guise well into modern times.

Cake offerings were often Christianised, usually by marking them with a cross (e.g. Hot Cross Buns) although if we look closely we can sometimes spot clues to earlier heathen origins. For example, St Hubert was the patron saint of hunters, particularly popular in the Netherlands where St Hubert Cakes (oblong and marked with a cross) were taken to Church and blessed. Dogs and horses – animals associated with Woden - were also taken to church for a blessing, suggesting St Hubert's festival on the 3rd November could have replaced an earlier one around the same time dedicated to the heathen god. (De Cleene 2003 Vol 2:109)

In Europe, St Martin of Tours' festival on November 11th was marked with St Martin Horns or cake figures (sometimes mounted on a horse) on a stick. In Brussels people baked bird shaped cakes, possibly intended to represent the raven, and these again were speared on sticks. The combination of birds, horses and sticks or spears strongly suggests the festival was originally dedicated to Woden.

On December 6th, St Nicholas' Day was celebrated in northern Europe with cakes resembling early drawings of Woden where the Bishop's mitre replaces the god's helmet, while the crozier replaces his spear.

Woden was also associated with bread. In Schleswig-Holstein in Germany, it was customary to shut the door while making bread in case Woden and the Wild Hunt passed by. Otherwise his dogs, who were particularly partial to a portion of uncooked dough, would swarm in through open doors and scoff the lot!

Heathen Yule cakes could have been easily Christianised by placing crosses on them. We also know that cakes and breads remained popular during the Christian Twelfth Night festivities. It is possible – although not provable – that the three Kings replaced an early trinity of gods, goddesses or heroes especially when we consider that Yule, too, was celebrated over twelve nights.

Traditionally the specially-baked Twelfth Night cake contained a bean (and sometimes also a pea). Whoever had the slice containing the bean became Bean King, while (in England) whoever had the pea became the Bean Queen. Although we lack written records for this tradition for more than a few centuries, it may well have been practised long before being committed to writing.

Some believe Lord Barleycorn and Lady Bean in the north of England were regarded as servants of the fertility god Frey, although this is difficult to either prove or disprove (Chaney 1962). Gerald Gardner claimed that the modern 'Lucky Pig' was the direct descendant of Frey's Boar, and that originally placing a boar device on an Anglo-Saxon helmet would deflect sword cuts. (Gardner 1942:97). During Yule it was traditional to sacrifice a wild boar to the god Frey.

Christian saints such as St Anthony Abbot whose feast days fall around this time of year seem to share many attributes of their earlier, heathen counterparts. For example, St Anthony Abbot was associated with pigs, which might explain why he was chosen to replace the heathen got Frey. However the saint could also be linked to Woden because the saint used to feed ravens while he lived as a hermit in the desert and Woden/Odin was traditionally associated with ravens. It is entirely possible there was once a festival dedicated to Woden at this time of year.

The similarities between some north European and Anglo-Saxon celebrations are intriguing. For example, in Belgium, the feast of the Conversion of St Paul on 25th January was celebrated with small cakes of rye and salt which were either given to cattle to keep them healthy or buried in each corner of the field. This has similarities with the Anglo Saxon Land Remedy Charm or *Æcerbot* (Grendon 1909:173). Burying cakes suggests a magical intention to make the land fertile by magically feeding it or by making an offering to placate one of the earth deities, such as Nerthus. Possibly there was a now lost tradition of burying cakes in Anglo-Saxon England on certain dates of the year to ensure fertility in the year ahead.

Chapter Twelve

Amulets and charms

We know the Anglo-Saxons used amulets because the Church regularly denounced their use. Bede calls them 'the false remedies of idolatry' (EHEN IV: 27) and one of the Canons present at the Synod of Clofeshoh in 747CE declared that amulets were among the 'errors of the heathen.' (Wilson 1992 :38)

Magically, amulets work through a sympathetic association of ideas, using plants, bones, teeth, skin, precious and common stones or anything considered sacred to an appropriate deity or spirit. Some amulet-like artefacts have been found in Anglo-Saxon graves, especially those of women. According to Tacitus, Germanic women possessed an 'element of holiness and prophecy' (Germania: 8). This could explain why early Christian Penitentials were particularly harsh in their attitudes towards women who practised magic and divination.

Other amulet-like objects found in early Anglo-Saxon burials include cowrie shells. These would have originated from the Red Sea and even from further east suggesting there was some trade with England. Cowrie shells were associated with fertility because the opening was thought to resemble the female sexual organs. These shells turn up in numerous burials of the seventh century, just at a time when England was apparently converting *en masse* to Christianity. They are most common in the burials of children and women and often worn as pendants or carried in wooden containers with other amulets. (Wilson 1992:104) In fact the Anglo-Saxon *þweng*, (meaning a thong) was another word for amulet, and strongly suggests that many were worn around the neck (Pollington 2003:422).

Many things we take for granted nowadays, such as perfume or jewellery all had their origins in protective magic. For example, Grave 299 at Kingston Down in Kent, contained a cowrie and a limpet shell, a silver brooch, two spindlewhorls, a pebble, four pieces of ivory, an ivory comb and a small bell in a wooden box (Godfrey-Faussett 1856:92). Although we cannot know exactly how these items were used, nor what they represented, they are curiously reminiscent of a paragraph in the (much later) writings of Burchard: '...have you clapped together over a corpse the combs which little women use to tease wool?' (Paragraph 83) This suggests a funerary ritual now lost to us that may well have been practised in England in Anglo-Saxon times.

Naturally cremations destroyed most of the grave offerings. However, sometimes antler Combs were placed in cremation after the body had been burned. These are not real combs. Often they are either too small to have been used, or the teeth are blunt or not properly cut, suggesting they were included for ritual purposes only or that they had a magical function. From a practical point of view, placing objects in the urn after cremation meant they could not be lost on the pyre.

Equally intriguing is the deliberate breaking of items before being placed in the pots. There must surely have been a magical purpose to this. Perhaps it was intended to prevent their use in magic or ritual (especially hexing) or to discourage theft by making them unusable. The idea that items belonging to the dead were magically empowered is supported in Burchard, (Paragraph 83) where priests are directed to ask whether they anyone has, '...tied a dead man's belt in knots in order to harm someone.'

Although amber amulets were popular, they melted during cremation, and therefore only survived in burials or by being placed in the pot after cremation. Amber amulets are often found in the graves of women and children, although occasionally they were also used to protect a man's sword or scabbard (Wilson 1992:112).

Amethyst beads were found almost exclusively in female burials, and were believed to ensure good health. Placing them in a grave suggests it was felt the dead still could suffer ill health in the afterlife. Male burials often included iron pyrites (Fool's Gold), sometimes alongside an iron strike-a-light and flints. Possibly it was hoped such items would help the deceased light his way from the grave to the afterlife. If this was the magical reasoning behind such items, then it indicates an Anglo-Saxon belief in a journey after death in order to reach the afterlife. It could also explain why rock crystal beads were sometimes placed in the deceased's hand since quartz is often associated with fire, light and healing. Crystal balls have been found in female graves dating from the late fifth to the early seventh century, especially in Kent (Wilson 1992:113).

Knot magic or *ligatura* were popular (and condemned by the early Church) right across Europe, and it seems likely the Anglo-Saxons practised something similar. However since knots are usually tied in perishable materials (string, leather and even grass) the evidence is easily lost. Even if something survives it is almost impossible to prove a magical connection. After all, a magical knot looks very much like any other sort of knot!

Knots were not only tied in twine, but also in cloth. Burchard condemned these as 'nefarious bandages' or *ligamenta* (Paragraph 54). Tying such knots in order to heal one's own livestock or hex those belonging to someone else was said to be accompanied by 'diabolical formulae.' Afterwards they were either hidden in trees or thrown into the centre of a crossroads. Similar spells could also be said over bread or grass.

Although we cannot be sure what sort of knot magic – if any – was performed by the Anglo-Saxons, 'nefarious bandages' could very well describe rag trees and rag wells where offerings of cloth were made, usually to obtain healing. Many of these are still in use today.

One of the main reasons why knot magic was so widely condemned was because it could be used to cause male impotence and/or infertility. In the Anglo Saxon Charms (Grendon 1909:201), a cure for headaches also claims to cure sexual constriction. Magically this was caused by tying knots. Up until one hundred and fifty years ago, brides and grooms would still undo the fastenings on their clothes before the ceremony to ensure no knot magic could harm them.

The Church also prohibited setting up wreaths at any crossroads cross. As we have seen, magical knots or bandages were sometimes thrown into the centre of a crossroads which were traditionally regarded as powerful sites. Suicides and those who had been hanged were often buried at crossroads, so possibly such wreaths were intended to placate the souls of the dead (McNeill 1933:462).

Sometimes it is not clear whether items found in graves were really amulets at all. For example, wooden and cylindrical copper boxes (known variously as amulet, relic or even work boxes) have been found in women's graves. Copper boxes were often worn from a woman's girdle and some contained pieces of cloth. Although it seems likely such curious items had some magical, healing or religious function, we simply cannot be sure what that was.

Cremation pots also provide interesting clues about the religious and magical beliefs and practices of the Anglo-Saxons. Some are pierced with 'ghost holes,' perhaps to enable communication with the dead. Alternatively, they may have allowed the deceased's spirit to be released or enabled libations to poured onto the remains on special feast days. Occasionally ghost holes have been sealed with lead, which suggests either an attempt to repair accidental damage, or some other addition to the funerary ritual. Fifth century urns sometimes contained windows, perhaps to enable the dead to observe the living (Wilson 1992: 141).

Even if we cannot be certain how ghost holes were supposed to work, the deceased's relatives clearly felt they were important and should be included. At some point a conscious decision was taken to bury or cremate the dead in a certain way and with (or without) certain goods. These decisions would have reflected their religious, cultural or magical beliefs. For example, items are often broken before being placed in cremation urns (but rarely in a grave). This could have represented the ritual 'death' of items belonging to or associated with the deceased. The different practices between burial and cremation however remains intriguing.

Likewise, decisions were made whether and how to decorate cremation urns, and which grave goods to include. Male burials were often accompanied by swastikas which were the symbol of Thunor, and often combined with lightning symbols and zigzags. Swastikas and the **t** rune are sometimes engraved on spear heads and swords. The Holborough Spear for instance has two runes, with the Tiw rune (thought to represent victory) on top facing upwards and the Ur rune (possibly representing strength) below. The small size of such symbols is interesting because it implies they were intended only to empower the bearer of the weapon and not to strike fear into the enemy.

Although nowadays most people would avoid wearing a swastika at all costs, it was extremely popular among the Anglo-Saxons, either as a decorative symbol or as the shape of a brooch. Sometimes this took the shape of 'running legs' which was particularly popular on the saucer shaped brooches worn by young women and girls.

There may also be a link between incised swastika decorations and crystals. In European folklore, rock crystal was sometimes known as a thunderstone (Simpson 1979:97) suggesting a possible link between Thunor, god of thunder, and his symbol, the swastika.

Of course grave goods may have links with several different deities. For example, the boar was often associated with Frey, and it features on helmets such as the Sutton Hoo helmet, but boars could also associated with Woden. Boar's teeth were also worn as pendants or simply placed in graves especially those of women, perhaps for the purposes of fertility or protection.

According to Tacitus (Germania:45) the Aestii worshipped the Mother of the Gods, and wore '...as emblems of this cult, the masks of boars,' instead of armour. It is therefore possible that boar symbols had similar associations for the Anglo-Saxons too.

A wide range of animal teeth accompanied burials. Female graves in particular sometimes contain pendants made of dog and beaver teeth. Wealthy burials sometimes had beaver teeth set in gold. An Anglo Saxon charm to cure a swelling recommends a fox's tooth wrapped in a fawn's skin (Grendon 1909:201). Teeth from carnivorous animals may have been intended to protect the wearer, yet this does not explain why ox teeth were also so popular. Possibly they represented strength.

Fossils were also placed in graves. Sometimes they have been pierced, suggesting they were worn as pendants although holes also had a magical purpose. For example, for centuries ordinary holed stones were said to have the power to prevent attacks by the Night-mare. Stones appear in several of the Anglo-Saxon charms and were often kept in houses for good luck or to ward off evil spirits (Grendon 1909: 134). We also know that Anglo-Saxons worshipped stones from the ancient laws found in the canons of King Cnut, King Edgar and also in the penitentials (Thorpe 1840).

Various coloured stones were also popular amulets and in some cases the colour corresponds to the magical intention. For example, sailors carried blue stones, washing them in order to change the winds (Grimm 1842 Vol III:185) while white stones protected the wearer against a stitch (the plant stitchwort has white flowers), lightning, thunder, and delusions (Grendon 1909:154).

Stones could be either carried on one's person, or kept either indoors or outside. The famous Anglo-Saxon Field Remedy charm advises farmers to take a meal stone, cover it in certain inscriptions and then place it in the middle of a field in order to protect his land.

Amulets also consisted of written formulae – usually on a strip of parchment but sometimes written directly onto the body. The use of writing suggests a small group of literate people (including, possibly, some priests) ministering to the magical needs of their community. It is of course possible to copy a formula without knowing what it means, while in heathen Anglo-Saxon society, the formulae may have consisted only of symbols.

It is only a very short step from marking weapons and tools with protective sigils to empowering them specifically for magical use. Then as now, many magical tools were made from organic materials such as wood and leather which have since perished, or become impossible to recognise in their proper context. For example, a length of wood may now only be regarded as evidence that people used a staff – which is common enough when people walk a great deal. However the archaeological record cannot tell us whether the staff was used *only* for walking or whether it had other, more esoteric purposes.

For example, one Anglo-Saxon charm for a journey states, 'I protect myself with this rod' (Grendon 1909: 177). The first part of the charm reads:

> *I protect myself with this rod, and commend myself to the grace of God,*
>
> *Against the grievous stitch, against the fire stroke of disease,*
>
> *Against the gruesome horror,*
>
> *Against the frightful terror loathsome to all men,*
>
> *Against all evil too, that may invade this land.*
>
> *A victory–charm I chant, a victory rod I bear,*
>
> *Word victory and work victory. May they potent be:*
>
> *That no nightmare demon vex me nor belly fiend afflict me,*
>
> *Nor ever for my life fear come upon me.*

Apart from providing a vivid image of the type of magical attacks expected by the average Anglo-Saxon traveller, this charm records ownership of a powerful magical tool. What it does not tell us however is how such power was acquired. The type of wood is not specified, and we do not know whether it had to be magically empowered. Normally however, a rod retains its bark whereas a wand is peeled. 'Word victory' could have mean an inscription (possibly runic) or oral formula, while 'work victory' suggests some sort of ritual. Although we do not have the details, the power in the words, even now, suggests it must have been a spectacular magical performance.

Chapter Thirteen

Variety in Magic

P

eople often imagine that Anglo Saxon magic consisted of little more than a few muttered words or a hastily made amulet. Actually Anglo Saxon culture – as we can see from the wonderful metalwork that has survived – was highly sophisticated. Also we know that later 'Wise Women' and 'Cunning Men' engaged in quite sophisticated shamanic practices, (Wilby 2010:6) so it is quite possible the Anglo-Saxons practised something similar.

There is also evidence that some people were thought to possess special powers, and 'potent women' were singled out as particularly fearsome (Magoun 1947:36). Even to be blessed and lucky was considered proof of innate magical power. In the well-known Land Remedy Charm (also known as the Acerbot or Æcerbot) (Grendon 1909: 173), a landowner wishing to ensure the fertility of his fields is directed to pray 'That no witch so artful, nor seer so cunning be [That e'er] may overturn the words hereto pronounced.'

Of course most of us only read these charms as translations, which can vary a great deal. For example, a line in a charm 'Against a sudden stitch' has been translated both as 'It hath fled there to the mountains; no respite hath it had,'(Grattan 1927:2) and also as 'Yonder to the mountain flee [hag, who sent the dart!' (Grendon 1909: 167) Even if the meaning seems clear, we may still not fully understand it unless we can somehow get into the mindset of the charm's original creators. We are, after all, modern people living in the twenty-first century, not sixth century Anglo-Saxons!

Their outlook and ways of thinking were quite different from ours. For example, they paid great attention to the natural world around them and learned to interpret its messages, because it helped ensure their survival. They used incantations and rituals, they shouted at the moon from time to time, and they sacrificed animals as part of their religious rituals, eating the meat afterwards. They believed that spells could cure while looks could kill and the early   Church had a hard time indeed trying to persuade them otherwise.

At first sight the difference between spells and prayers is not always clear. The Church taught that prayers worked if God permitted but that this could not be forced (Rowlatt 2001:207) Spells, however, attempted to coerce supernatural forces and would work if they were properly performed. Many spells and charms also invoked deities (including the Christian God and saints) as part of the ritual. Healers or leeches regularly performed magic to heal their patients.

Sometimes clues lie in the words. For example in religious poetry the term *searo* was often applied to those who opposed God.   However it can have many other meanings, including snare, trap or even armour *(searonet)* , a construction *(searoband)*, to create *(syrwan)*, fetters or bonds *(searo)*, cunning *(nearosearo)*, mystery or secret *(searoþanc)*, treasure or ornaments *(searogimmas)* and magical purity *(searohwit)* (Taylor 1983:115-6).

This suggests that weapons, armour and even chains were closely inter-linked and all were associated with magic. In fact, Riddle 23, Line 16 of the Exeter Riddle Book, has *searosaeled* meaning a key, another object closely associated with locks and magic. Likewise in Beowulf (line 2764) the dragon's treasure includes arm rings that have been *searwum gesæled*, suggesting either that they have been cursed or that they are intended as a protective ornament.

This also sheds some light on Bede's famous story of Imma, who was captured by one of Æthelred's earls and chained up to prevent his escape (Bede EHEN IV: 22). Imma's brother Tunna was a priest and when he heard (wrongly as it happened) that Imma had been killed, he went looking for his body. Unfortunately he identified the wrong body, which he took back to bury in his monastery, and said many masses for his soul.

According to Bede, these masses caused Imma's chains to keep falling off and his captor, the earl, enquired whether he had any spells (some versions say runes) about him , '...as are spoken of in fabulous stories.' Clearly there was some longstanding Anglo-Saxon magical tradition of binding and unbinding even though Bede has Imma insist that he was freed only by his brother's prayers and masses.

When it suited him however, Bede could believe in magic as well as the next man. In EHEN Book I:1 he mentions how jet '...is black and sparkling, glittering at the fire, and when heated, drives away serpents...' The Anglo-Saxons traditionally associated fire with treasure, and the Anglo-Saxon rune *sigel* (meaning sun) was also linked with the derivatives *sigle* and *sigli* both meaning treasure. In particular this could mean treasure in the form of a protective necklace (Taylor 1983:119). Also, returning to Bede's comment about the serpents, this could also refer to dragons who were well known treasure guardians.

Horde is another popular word associated with treasure and is probably related linguistically to *heord* meaning hair. In Norse culture hair represented fertility, so plaited loaves of bread could represent a link between the treasure of wheat, and the fertility of the harvest. Possibly the Anglo-Saxons had a similar tradition.

Some common words found in modern paganism and neo-paganism have their origins in Anglo-Saxon. For example *wicce* meaning a witch or sorcerer while 'the Craft' comes from *cræft* meaning strength. Along with *mægen* 'power' and *miht* meaning 'might' these three words often occur in the Anglo Saxon charms. *Cræft* is often combined with other words, including *scinn craeft*, meaning magical skill, *lybcraeft* meaning skill in using healing drugs.

Then there is g*aldor-craeft*, the chanting or singing of spells, together with *wiccecraeft* (witchcraft) and *bealocraeft* (sorcery). Witches were also sometimes called *wyrtgalstre* meaning a plant charmer (Pollington 2003: 469). In a society reliant upon oral traditions, *tungolcraeft* meaning skilled at reading words may have had a special, magical significance. Whereas the word *wig* is often associated with war, *wiglung* means divination, perhaps because it was practised before battle.

Such a wide vocabulary emphasises how important magic must have been in Anglo-Saxon life. Otherwise there would have been no need for precise words to convey specific types of magical work and ritual. Nowadays many people outwardly at least, pretend that magic does not exist; they do not specify which particular type of magic they are talking about and the word has become a generic expression.

Although the two terms, miracles and magic, are often used interchangeably, there is a subtle difference. Miracles are attributed to divine intervention while magic is usually credited to human intrusion. Early church writers often describe how miracles helped convert the heathen Anglo-Saxons although obviously their accounts are biased.

As we read the works of Bede and others, it seems the early Church missionaries found themselves locked in a game of one-upmanship with heathen magic and its practitioners. This resulted in a few far-fetched claims, for example, that Bishop Wilfrid had to teach people how to fish! Another example describes how the South Saxons had suffered from a three year drought in the late seventh century. Only when they were converted (again by Wilfrid) did it rain again (both examples from Bede EHEN IV: 13)

At first sight, what Bede described was a miracle and nothing more. However, we know from Burchard of Worms that the Germanic peoples of northern Europe (especially the women) practised weather magic. Now obviously what Burchard is describing may never have travelled across the English Channel with the migrating Anglo-Saxons. On the other hand, folk magic is surprisingly mobile. It is therefore worth examining what Burchard said in more detail.

In paragraph 180, Burchard describes in great detail how women would 'gather together many young girls and put one small virgin in charge as their leader.' Naked, the girl was taken to a place outside the village where henbane grew. She then dug up the plant using the little finger of her right hand and tied it to the little toe of her right foot.

Dragging the plant behind her, she then walked into a nearby river, followed by other girls who each carried a single branch. At the river they all dipped their branches into the water and sprinkled this onto the young girl who then returned to her village. 'By their incantations' thundered Burchard, 'they thereby hope to get rain.'

This is another good example of the double standards of the time. Weather magic practised by women was condemned, but when Christian clergy such as Wilfrid brought the rain it was a miracle. Once again, it seems what the church really objected to was ordinary people having any sort of independent magical powers. The fact the Church focussed so harshly on women, suggests that in pre-Christian times, women could have been the caretakers of magical lore and practice.

Bede's account of Wilfrid bringing the rain could also have been a sanitised account of a magical battle between Anglo-Saxon weather-mongers and Christian clergy. The missionaries did not always win and even Bede sometimes resorted to claiming that plagues were impossible to stop because they were sent by God.

Occasionally we come across some really intriguing ideas, for example that inanimate objects could commit criminal acts. If a fire destroyed trees then the fire was regarded as a thief, and whoever lit the fire was also guilty and fined. However, if that same person took an axe and cut down half the forest, then he was only liable to pay for three of the trees he cut. This was because the axe was regarded as an informer, but not a thief (Bonser 1946:7). The Anglo-Saxons clearly regarded the difference as important.

It was certainly believed that inanimate objects interacted with people and animals with which they had recently been in close contact. For example, charms to recover animals and goods had to be sung over items that had been closely associated with them. For example, if a horse went missing then the charm was sung over its bridle. With missing cattle it had to be sung over the imprints of their hoofprints, while dripping hot candlewax three times into the indentations. The magical thinking behind this must have been that as it cooled and solidified, the wax would 'fix' the animals in one spot until they could be recovered.

The ever-practical Anglo Saxons recognised however that an ounce of protection is worth a ton of cure, so protective remedies against theft were also used. To prevent the theft of bees – a valuable commodity at a time when honey was the only viable source of sweetness – the owner was directed to place 'a plant of madder on thy hive, then no one will lure away thy bees, nor can they be stolen while the plant is on the hive."(quoted in Bonser 1946:11)

Of course it is one thing to read a charm, but quite another to have seen it performed at the time. It can be helpful at this point to compare the Anglo-Saxon Charms with remarks in some Christian writings. For example, Burchard (paragraph 155) tells priests to ask whether penitents have used herbs, words, wood, gemstones - all popular ingredients in Anglo-Saxon charms.

Penitents were also asked whether they had anything concealed in their mouths, sewn into their clothing or tied about the body. This is interesting because such methods were not only used in the Anglo-Saxon charms but have survived in folk magic all over northern Europe, some right up into the late nineteenth and early twentieth century. Presumably most penitents denied involvement in such things but went on practising them anyway.

Of course the early Church was not only concerned with people's actions but also their beliefs. For example, it was held a sin to believe that certain types of magic were possible whether or not you actually practised them. It was also claimed that some people could kill baptised people without using any weapons, cook their flesh, eat it, put straw or wood in place of their hearts and then bring them back to life again! (Burchard paragraph 159)

Even if you personally never attempted anything so gross, the Church taught that just believing that it *might* be possible was a sin in itself. Yet it was the Church who taught that these things happened. Much later, many of these allegations of magical malpractice became the staple allegations of the witch-hunters and Inquisition.

From these examples we can see how the early Church created a climate of fear. They taught that people flew through the sky at night, with 'other minions of the devil' and subsequently fought amongst the clouds, although quite why they did this remained a mystery. Whether this was already part of heathen belief, or a Christian invention to frighten people into orthodoxy, we cannot be certain.

Another thing we can learn from the various early Church authors is their antagonism towards women. It is tempting to assume this must have been because heathen women had traditionally been in charge of certain rituals, rites of passage and healing. Although none of the penitential authors claims to have witnessed heathen rituals personally, they often include so much detail that it sounds as though they must have - at least until you examine their claims more closely.

For example, it is difficult to imagine any priest standing idly by as a woman took off her clothes, covered her body in honey and then rolled back and forth on the ground over a sheet spread with wheat (Burchard, paragraph 179). The wheat that stuck to the body was then collected and ground into flour with the mill being turned 'in the opposite direction of the sun.' This flour was then made into bread and given to the husband to eat with the intention of making him 'grow weak and die'.

Now admittedly Burchard may have been relying on gossip here, but anyone who has ever tried to grind flour will know it is almost impossible to do if the grains are covered in honey! Bearing this in mind, perhaps we should take similar claims, e.g. that women could steal their neighbours' milk or honeybees, cast the evil eye on animals by using words, looks or sounds, and travel at night through closed doors (Paragraphs 156-8) with a very large pinch of salt.

Some spells are so bizarre, we have to wonder whether the Church actually had any evidence or whether it was purely erotic wishful thinking. For example, women were banned from keeping live fish in their vaginas. Once dead the fish was cooked and given to the husband to eat as a love spell! (Burchard Paragraph 160) Another charm involved the woman lying face down on the ground while someone else kneaded bread on her bare buttocks. The dough was then cooked and given to the husband to eat (Paragraph 161). Even menstrual or animal blood was included in magical ingredients along with a tonic drink made from another man's burned skull (Paragraphs 164, a and b) Did these activities really take place or were they completely – or partially – invented by the Church authorities?

Although it is tempting to dismiss everything as the work of overwrought imaginations, some things described by Burchard and his ilk were still being practiced in Europe and England almost into living memory.

For example, he describes how women 'dig a hole in the ground and make a tunnel through to the other side; then they pull their baby through the hole and say that this stops the baby's crying' (paragraph 165). Since babies tend to cry when they are unwell, this was probably part of a healing ritual. Pulling the sick through holes in the ground and hoops of bramble for healing and protection certainly continued into the early twentieth century.

Obviously it would be foolish to try and claim an unbroken link from the nineteenth century back to Burchard and then into seventh century Anglo-Saxon England. but the similarities are surely strong enough to make us sit up and take some notice.

Sometimes remarks in the penitentials echo practices in the Anglo-Saxon charms. We have already noticed spells sung over footprints in order to recover stolen livestock, while Burchard (Paragraph 163) claims that women used earth from a Christian's footprint in order to harm him. Clearly the magical thinking in both cases was that the earth in the footprint retained a psychic link with the person who originally made the mark and that this could be magically manipulated.

Many household tasks could easily be adapted for magical purposes. Burchard particularly condemns the 'incantations and counter-incantations of women over their webs,' while 'uttering incantations before 'wool-work or weaving' [paragraph 55] The association of weaving with destiny is very ancient, and is found almost two millennia earlier in Homer's Odyssey. Indeed the Anglo-Saxon word *gewaef* meaning wove is closely linked with the word *gewif* meaning fortune.

Burchard also mentions the practice of beginning tasks such as winding thread, spinning and sewing, and 'doing all the work they can begin' on the 'holy night' of the eighth day after the Nativity (January 1st) (paragraph 92). This implies that particular dates (not just moonphases) were considered lucky for starting certain tasks, especially those usually done by women.

Of course Burchard's dates may have been associated with Roman rather than Germanic traditions. However Anglo-Saxon women certainly spun and wove cloth and buried spindle whorls in graves. It would be very unusual for them not to have some superstitions about the best times to begin or complete such work.

Several penitentials condemn celebrating during an eclipse of the moon. Although the descriptions of words and actions are sketchy and may have varied from place to place, we do know the celebrations were intended to obtain protection. They were often accompanied by jugglers and chanting diviners. We also know the practice was hard to eradicate because Burchard was still condemning them in the eleventh century.

Moon phases seem to have been important in magic and ritual all over northern Europe, where the new moon considered the best time for new beginnings such as building a house or getting married. All the small rituals we have connected with new moons – turning over the change in our pocket for 'good luck,' or even bowing to the moon, for example, may not have originated with the Anglo-Saxons but certainly seems to have been observed by them.

Chapter Fourteen

Divination and Curses

D

ivination has been practised all over the world, especially whenever life is difficult or uncertain. The Church was hostile towards divination from earliest times yet provides clues about the commonest methods. Ælfric (Lives of Saints, Book 1:17 *De Auguriis*) for example, stated, 'He who trusteth in auguries, either from birds, or from sneezing is, either from horses, or from dogs, he is no Christian but is an infamous apostate.' Harsh words, but largely ignored. Even nowadays, people still count flower petals or apple pips, showing that divination was peculiarly resistant to Christian attempts to abolish it. This was probably because it answered a deep-seated need in a way that nothing else could. Then as now, people need certainty in an uncertain world.

We cannot help wondering how the early Church authors obtained their information about some magical practices. Presumably no-one would be rash enough to do anything remotely magical in front of a Christian priest. This suggests people were encouraged to spy on friends, family and neighbours and report on the smallest departure from permitted religious practice. Such things happened – for a different ideology – in Stalin's Russia.

Burchard, writing centuries after Ælfric, describes people placing barley grains in front of the fire and watching them closely. If the barleycorns jumped it foretold danger ahead, but if they remained still there would be peace. Fortune telling using grains and nuts on a fire remained popular right up into the middle of the twentieth century in the UK. With the loss of open fires however, it finally faded from memory. Yet divination was never really eradicated, despite the clergy's warning, 'Do not seek by lots to discover what will happen to you.' (Griffiths, 1996:145)

We know the Anglo-Saxons practised divination by birds and omens because both Theodore's Penitential and the Synod of Clofeshoh in 747 ordered bishops to prohibit '...pagan practices, that is divinations, fortune telling by casting lots, from the flight of birds, from watching birds, amulets, incantations' (Haddan and Stubbs 1871:364).

The Church was not above interpreting an omen or two when it suited them, however. The anonymous life of St Gregory written by a Whitby monk between 680 and 714 tells how Edwin of Northumbria was on his way to church with his attendants 'when a crow with a strident voice sounded an evil omen' (Whitelock 1955:688). The saint's rather unkind response was to shoot the bird with an arrow, perhaps to prevent anyone present from interpreting it as an omen against himself.

In Northern Europe, according to Burchard, great attention was paid to the behaviour of animals and birds. When setting out on a journey it was considered a good omen if a crow croaked from somewhere over to your left (McNeill 1933:463). Burchard also claimed that people feared to leave their homes before daybreak because it was 'forbidden to go out before the cock crows' (Paragraph 138). This shows how persistent some beliefs can be, since even today some believe that the dawn crowing of a cockerel drives evil away.

Birds were not only used in divination, but also in magic. An Anglo-Saxon protection charm to be performed before a fight recommends cooking swallows, either in wine or spring water and then eating them (Grendon 1909:137). Magically it may have been felt whoever ate the birds would assume their speed and agility. In much the same way, Anglo-Saxons believed the flesh or body parts of badgers, dogs, wolves, porpoises, goats, and sheep could not only cure disease but also grant extra strength or protection (Cockayne 1864 Vol I:70ff).

Bede mentions something called the *Sortes Sanctorum*, a collection of religious works that were used for divination. Basically you opened the book, (which could include the Bible) and interpreted the first words you saw as the answer to your question. Even though the source of the oracle was undoubtedly Christian, the early church, including St Augustine, strongly condemned the practice as did Burchard. The Frankish penitential even made it an offence to revere the *Sortes Sanctorum*, let alone consult it (McNeill 1933:456). Yet many people – even those who would describe themselves as practising Christians – continued to use some form of *sortes* right up into the nineteenth century.

Bede's condemnation of divination by *Sortes* raises some interesting questions. Most ordinary people in England during the entire Christian and heathen Anglo-Saxon period were illiterate – apart from the clergy. Ordinary people – even wealthy ones - would not have had access to valuable hand-written manuscripts which were kept chained in churches and monasteries.

This means that those who performed the *Sortes Sanctorum* were almost certainly Christian clergy. Human nature being what it is, they might even have charged a fee to do it! This really is not such an outrageous idea. After all, many early medieval trials for occult practices were actually of priests, not laymen. As late as the Middle Ages, anyone accused of a crime could claim 'benefit of the clergy' if they could read, which allowed them to be tried more leniently than a lay person.

Another method of divination involved interpreting patterns and shapes made by connecting random points on the earth's surface, or looking for patterns in a handful of seed, grains, or dust that had been thrown haphazardly. The most common figures were squares, rectangles, triangles, circles, and pentagrams.

Curses

Since the heathen Anglo-Saxons relied wholly on oral tradition, all written legal documents and edicts etc., belong to the later Christian period after c.600 CE until just before the Norman conquest in 1066 CE. Even long after the English converted to Christianity, true literacy was restricted to a small number of clerics.

However meanings have changed. Then, 'to write' actually meant to dictate to a scribe, while 'to read' meant listening to listen to someone else (almost certainly a cleric) reading aloud. Legal documents were created after first being orally enacted. They were then read aloud for approval, with the scribe marking a cross or writing the name on the document which the witness then touched either with a finger or a dry pen (Earle 1888:36-37).

We could easily be forgiven for assuming we will never find any examples of Anglo-Saxon curses. Yet we do, and it's not just the occasional example, but a whole raft of them especially in Wills. They range from the simple, 'And whoever alters this, may God turn His face from him on the Day of Judgment...' (Whitelock 1986:95 *Will of Sifted*) to the more elaborate demand that god should deliver the culprit, '...into the abyss of hell to Satan the devil and all his accursed companions and there suffer with God's adversaries without end and never trouble my heirs.' (Whitelock 1986:87 *Will of Wulfgyth*)

It seems highly unlikely that legal curses originated with Christianity even though God is often invoked as a supernatural power and there are certainly curses in the Bible. What seems to have happened is that curses were grafted onto pre-existing traditions. We have to remember that originally legal documents were enacted orally – including the curses. They were not simply added on when the document was written up later.

One vivid account describes a group of high ranking clergy, lead by Archbishop Wulfhelm, participating in one such curse. Whoever contradicted the terms of the land grant document was to be '...cut off and hurled into the abyss of hell for ever without end. And all the people who stood by said "So be it, Amen, Amen."' (Robertson 1956:44-45)

Although officially the Church frowned on people cursing their neighbours, legal documents seem to have been a different matter. There the curse was framed to include the promise of punishment from God and excommunication from the Church. For example, a land grant by King Edgar, 958 A.D. threatens, 'May the Almighty God lessen his days in this world.'(Whitelock 1979: 558) Even so, some curses remained curiously secular. For example, a land grant by Æthelheard King of Wessex in 739 AD simply states 'Whoever diminishes or alters it, may his joy be turned into sorrow.' (Whitelock 1979:496)

It does not seem likely that it was the Christian Church that invented the idea of adding curses to legal documents although they did put them in writing for the first time. More likely the primary oral re-enactment was a heathen tradition, and this included curses on those who broke the original contracts.

Certainly the Church was quick to make use of such curses however. Even books – which were all hand written and thus extremely valuable – often carried curses to protect them from theft and destruction. As late as the early Middle Ages, books were still chained up in Cathedral libraries for safe-keeping!

A word on the Runes...

At this point it may seem curious that the Anglo-Saxon rune poem has not been mentioned since the Anglo-Saxons certainly had a runic alphabet which became particularly useful for supplying those sounds absent from the

Roman alphabet. So the runes Þ (thorn) and **W** (wynn) often appear in Anglo Saxon manuscripts alongside the Latin alphabet in order to accommodate the 'th' and 'w' sounds respectively.

However, we have little information about whether the Anglo-Saxons used runes for divination in Anglo-Saxon times. They practised divination, yes. They had runes which they used in protective magic. Modern pagans/heathens may use Anglo-Saxon runes for divination. But we have no information that they were for divination by the Anglo-Saxons.

The only surviving copy of the Anglo-Saxon Rune poem dates from the early eighteenth century, and the rune signs and names appear to have been added later. Although linguistically, it may date from c. eleventh century or even earlier, we cannot be sure how much is original (Dickins 1915: 6). Nor do we know for certain whether the poem was meant to be a list of meanings specifically intended to aid divination or whether it was simply an aid to memorising the letters of the alphabet (rather like A is for Apple, B is for Book). Many important early English manuscripts were lost in a fire in 1731, and before many more had been used to clean brass candlesticks after the Dissolution of the Monasteries!

In looking for proof that runes were used for divination, it is tempting to hark back to Tacitus and his account of the Germanic tribes:

'They cut off a branch of a nut-bearing tree and slice it into strips; these they mark with different signs and throw them completely at random onto a white cloth. Then the priest of the state, if the consultation is a public one, or the father of the family if it is private, offers a prayer to the gods, and looking up at the sky picks up three strips, one at a time, and reads their meaning from the signs previously scored on them.' (Germania :10)

Yet nowhere in this passage is there any mention of runes. The Latin word Tacitus uses for 'signs' is *notae* which can mean 'signs' or 'letters.' 'Different signs' could mean almost anything.

This can be frustrating. Certainly the early Germanic tribes and the Anglo-Saxons engaged in divination, but Tacitus does not say they were using runes in order to do it. The divination method described in *The Germania* might have been using an altogether different system, now lost. Also Bede and other early authors do not mention divination by runes, although they mention other methods.

The Anglo Saxon Futhorc (since the fourth rune is 'oss' and the sixth is 'cen'. The Norse and Icelandic versions are called futharks)

There are a few additional runes from Northumbria, none of which appear in the Anglo-Saxon Rune poem. For the sake of completeness however they are given here:

The Anglo-Saxons certainly used runes in protective magic, especially on weapons. We also know they practiced divination, but we cannot say for sure that runes were used for this. The Norse tradition of course, used runes (the Elder and Younger futharks) in both divination and magic. Although there are many runic inscriptions in England, many of these date from after the Viking invasions.

Given the many similarities between the Anglo-Saxon and Norse traditions, it is possible the Anglo-Saxons used runes for divination. Yet the evidence to support this is happening in England relatively sparse. Even Bede and Gildas fail to mention it. For the time being therefore, we can only keep an open mind and keep looking for more evidence.

Chapter Fifteen

Christianising Magic

O

ften people are disappointed that the Anglo Saxon Charms are so heavily Christianised. Yet this is hardly surprising since they were written by monks, long after England had abandoned heathenism and become fervently Christian... or had it?

One thing we do know from Church writings is that the changeover to Christianity was by no means straight forward. There is evidence of much opposition and mind-changing even amongst the clergy. So the evidence should be treated with a certain amount of caution. Yes, some charms, especially those containing prayers, paternosters psalms, hymns, crosses, etc., *may* have originally contained Heathen equivalents. We can even speculate what these might have been. But ultimately none of this amounts to conclusive proof.

The reason I stress this is because this is one area where popular belief parts company with the academic world. Both sides have their bias and must often rely on what cannot be proved rather than what can. Yet with new information turning up every year, things may change dramatically in the next decade or two. And that is not a weakness, it's a strength, to realise where the problems really lie.

Some charms appear obviously heathen apart from the odd 'Amen' tacked on almost as an afterthought. Others contain many Christian phrases, or prayers such as the Paternoster. The famous Nine Herbs Charm (Grendon 1909 :191), which is very heathen in character, still includes Christian phrases including 'Herbs the Lord created, Holy in Heaven;' and 'Christ stood over venom' (although it also mentions Woden.) Still others balance out the Christian and heathen elements. A few are almost completely Christianised.

Before looking at some of the charms more closely, it is worthwhile briefly considering some comments by St Eligius, (588-659CE) an early Christian missionary who converted many Flemings, Frisians, Suevi, and the barbarian tribes along the European North Sea coast. Although he did not preach in England, St Eligius worked with people whose families may have recently emigrated to England. With their strong emphasis on family ties, it is possible they still regarded their relatives across the water as kinfolk.

Initially, Eligius sets out a list that reads very much like any other from that period. He condemns sorcerers, pagans, diviners and augury by sneezing and birds. Then he recommends that '...whether you are setting out on a journey, or beginning any other work, cross yourself in the name of Christ, and say the Creed and the Lord's Prayer with faith and devotion, and then the enemy can do you no harm. . .'(All quotes from Eligius come from Maitland 1841:50) Was he perhaps emphasising the changeover to trusting in Christ rather than some earlier, heathen deity? Possibly, although we cannot know for sure.

Eligius then continues, ' Let no Christian place lights at the temples, or the stones, or at fountains, or at trees, . . . or at places where three ways meet, or presume to make vows.' Here we see clearly how the natural world played a large part in the magical beliefs and practices of the European Germanic tribes.

However, his reference to temples is a little puzzling. According to Tacitus (writing several centuries earlier) the Germanic tribes held the natural world sacred and actively avoided temples. Perhaps by Eligius' time this had changed although we cannot be sure.

Eligius' comments about amulets is more revealing, condemning them '...even though they be made by the clergy, and called holy things, and contain the words of scripture.' This shows the real problem facing the early Church: their own clergy were combining Christianity with heathen beliefs and practices. We cannot help wondering just how devout some of the early priests actually were.

The Wessex-born St Boniface however leaves us in little doubt. He complained bitterly that the new (Christian) and ancient (heathen/pagan) rites had merged, and that 'foolish, reckless, or guilty priests are to blame' (Grimm 1842: Vol 1:75 note 3).

Of course, missionaries such as Eligius would have regarded even the most Christianised charm, full of Paternosters and Credos as thoroughly sinful. Ordinary people – and even some clergy – seem to have disagreed with him. Exhortations to trust only to God were all very well, but when things go badly people dislike feeling powerless. The charms – even when Christianised – gave people a certain amount of control over their lives. They could be performed at weddings, burials, to heal the sick, sung over bread, salt and honey (and even soft boiled eggs!) and upon houses, wells, orchards, cornfields, and over swords and battle standards.

Not all clergy were like Eligius. Some tried to make Christianity more accessible by combining it with the older heathen traditions. Clearly they could not banish the old beliefs and rituals altogether otherwise they would have done so. Meanwhile the Church swung between denying the existence of anything other than Christianity, and condemning heathen gods as demons. This created a few tensions.

For example, one charm against epilepsy directs that 'A mass priest shall perform this leechdom...' (Grendon 1909:146). This shows that in spite of the Church's official attitude, the clergy were often the ones performing these charms. They even made amulets, and practised tree, stone, and water charms. Despite claiming that all a sick person needed was prayer and sacraments, the Church still appointed official exorcists to banish the sickness demons. What could not be eradicated had to be accommodated and Christianised.

However this state of affairs did not last long. Eventually the Church became more hard line, punishing priests who performed incantations (as opposed to saying masses) for the dead. Although originally the Church had allowed the tradition of dancing during field and harvest celebrations to continue, this too became intolerable once nuns were reported dancing in a church. Theodore's Penitential expressly forbade it.

More amenable clergy sometimes found themselves in trouble. Even the late Anglo-Saxon cleric St Dunstan (909 – 988 CE) was accused of sorcery because he 'loved the vain songs of ancient heathendom, the trifling legends, the funeral chants.' (Gummere 1892:470)

As it is impossible to include every Anglo-Saxon charm in this book, I have chosen those that best illustrate certain types of magical thinking and show how they were constructed. Yet still there are gaps which can only be filled using educated guesswork. For example, some charms give instructions that they should be sung, but we do not know what type of melody or rhythms were used. Even some of the herbs are hard to identify with certainty.

Although at first glance many of the charms seem to have little in common, most contain at least one of the following nine characteristics:

> (1) Narrative introduction;
>
> (2) Appeal to a god or higher spirit;
>
> (3) Writing or speaking certain names or words of power;
>
> (4) An outline of how the disease demons will be dealt with;
>
> (5) The spell-caster's boast of power designed to terrify his   opponent/the demon;
>
> (6) Ceremonial directions to patient and exorcist;
>
> (7) Singing of incantations on parts of the body and on other objects;
>
> (8) The best time to perform the ritual (may be according to the time of day, moonphase etc.);
>
> (9) Sympathy and the association of ideas – the 'just as... so may' formula is one of the most common

Examining some of these features in a little more detail, we discover further patterns. For example, the Narrative introduction is sometimes also called the Epic Narrative. This technique is found in some of the earliest Indo-European charms, and appears in many and varied traditions around the world. Basically, the narrative describes great deeds performed by a god or hero (later saints or Christ), thus preparing the way for the rest of the spell. It works on the principle that something that can be done once in the past can be repeated here and now.

There are good examples of heathen narrative introductions in the two tenth century High German *Merseburger Zaubersprüche* where the Idisi (who were divine women, probably Valkyries) hover around a battlefield while the fighting continues, and helping favourite prisoners to escape.

In this particular example the narrative introduction takes up virtually the entire charm, with the actual spell formula 'Escape the bonds of captivity, flee from the foe!' only appearing in the final line (Fuller 1980:162). The spell appears very simple, but its power comes from the images in the narrative introduction that show the women 'settling down here and there.' Some were fastening fetters, others were picking them apart. What had been done in the past could therefore be repeated in the present.

In the second *Merseburger Zaubersprüche*, the gods Woden and Balder are out riding together and Balder's horse suffers a sprain. Three goddesses try unsuccessfully to heal it, and then Woden takes over and succeeds. Here it is the god mentioned in the narrative introduction who speaks the spell formula. Magically speaking, what works for the gods or heroes will work for man, and Woden's power is transferred to anyone subsequently using the charm.

As the Church began Christianising the charms, narrative introductions shift from stories about heathen gods and heroes to passages from the New Testament or anecdotes about Christ and his disciples. Woden is the only major deity to be invoked in any of the surviving charms, although there are references to other intriguing entities such as Erce or Noththe whose identities are now unknown. It seems likely saints, angels and the Trinity replaced earlier heathen entities and deities.

If we now turn to North European examples, we see some interesting results when heathenism became absorbed into Christianity. Wind elves were no longer invoked for help in storms, the *wazzer heilige* became equated with Christian saints invoked during storms, and semi-divine white robed women became Christianised as nuns (Grendon 1909:148)

In later Scandinavia, even Thor became equated Christ, who took over his role as conqueror of the mountain giants, and occupied a throne at the Norns' sacred fount (Meyer 1903:437). Blessings, once given with the sign of the hammer were replaced by the sign of the cross.

It is entirely possible – although not provable – that similar things had already happened in Anglo-Saxon England. Once again we find ourselves chasing the shadows...

Chapter Sixteen

The Land Remedy Charm

S

ometimes examining a charm in detail – even one that seems heavily Christianised – shows not only its basic structure but also how it might have been originally performed. The Land Remedy Charm, (Grendon 1909:173) intended to treat bewitched land, is a good example.

In our modern, mostly urban society it can be difficult to understand the importance our ancestors attached to the land. Yet seen through their eyes, it was perfectly understandable. The earth could nurture or destroy them so they must learn to work closely with it. Above all they must befriend it, so it would help them. In folk magic people were often dragged through tunnels in the earth or arches of turves for healing well into the nineteenth century.

Ploughed fields were considered particularly powerful. If you crossed three, seven or nine furrows and listened carefully you would hear the future being foretold. In some areas strangers were forbidden to cross the furrows, presumably to keep such knowledge of the future in the community or tribe!

The first part of the Land Remedy Charm sets how the ritual must be performed: at night, before daybreak, one of the most popular times to perform Anglo-Saxon magic. Next, the spell-caster must take four sods, one from each side of the land, (each is later to be returned to its exact spot).

Magically, the intention is that cleansing the turves will magically cleanse the entire area.

The spell also requires a collection of 'all known herbs', together with milk from cattle and twigs from every kind of soft-wood tree. These plus oil, honey and yeast are then placed on top of the cut turves. Since ploughing usually began straight after Yule/Christmas (Hutton 1996: 124) it must have been difficult to find so many herbs; perhaps there was a tradition of drying them for when they were needed.

The gathering of items symbolising the earth's fruitfulness is a form of sympathetic magic. The person casting the spell is showing that the earth in the field must be just as fruitful as the items placed on the turves, and this in turn removes any pre-existing bewitchment.

While assembling the ingredients the spell-caster had to recite the following: '*Crescite, et multiplicamini, et replete, terram,* meaning 'Grow, and multiply, and replenish, the earth'. Next he pronounced, *In nomine patris et filii et spiritus sancti sitis benedicti'* before reciting the Paternoster and sprinkling holy water three times on the earth as he did so. The original heathen formula probably used dew instead.

A priest then sang mass four times over the turves. This shows clear collusion between clergy, the person performing the spell and the land owner. Although the charms were copied out by monks, the official Church stance would certainly have condemned such magical practices. Despite its Latin incantations, this is still a very heathen charm. Yet it could not be performed without the complicity of a least one priest.

The landowner then had to obtain (or perhaps make) four aspen crosses. The choice of aspen wood is curious, since traditionally it was demonised as the wood used for the Crucifixion. This was so widely believed that sometimes people threw stones at aspen trees!

From a more practical point of view, aspen is interesting because its roots remain alive long after the tree itself dies. It can also send up suckers far from the parent tree. This might explain its enduring popularity in magic connected with death and the afterlife. In this case, the field's fertility had been magically killed and using aspen was a way of returning it to life again.

Next the four crosses were marked with the names of the Gospels, Mark, Luke, Matthew and John. Again, the use of writing suggests collusion with the clergy. Of course, the presence of crosses does not make this a uniquely Christian charm, since the cross shape also represents the much earlier sun wheel. In pre-Christian times, the four crosses may have been marked with suitable runes or other symbols but there is no real proof of this although the charm is a curious mixture of heathen actions and Christian words. The turves are placed on the crosses while repeating '*Crescite*' (grow) nine times – nine being one of the magical numbers.

Next the person performing the spell declares:

> *Eastward I stand, for blessings I pray,*
>
> *I pray the mighty Lord, I pray the potent Prince,*
>
> *I pray the holy guardian of the celestial realm,*
>
> *Earth I pray, and heaven above,*
>
> *And the just and saintly Mary,*
>
> *and Heaven's power and Temple high,*
>
> *that I, by grace of God, this spell*
>
> *May with my teeth dissolve; with steadfast will*
>
> *[May] raise up harvests for our earthly need,*
>
> *fill these meadows with a constant face,*
>
> *beautify these farm-turves; as the Prophet said*
>
> *that he on earth had favour to his alms*
>
> *apportioned wisely, obedient to God's will.*
>
> *Now I pray the Prince who shaped this world,*
>
> *That no witch so artful, nor seer so cunning be*

[That e'er] may overturn the words hereto pronounced. (Grendon 1909:175)

Obviously we cannot be certain whether earlier versions of the spell invoked heathen deities instead. If they did, we certainly cannot be certain who they were. It is possible however that 'Earth I pray' referred to an earth deity, and that Mary replaced a female Anglo-Saxon goddess.

The next part of the charm takes place when the first furrow is being ploughed. Obviously, the ploughing is a physical manifestation of the magic, showing the soil being overturned just as the original bewitching charm is being overturned, '*That no witch so artful, nor seer so cunning be... may overturn the words hereto pronounced.'* To this end, the spell-caster invokes a deity while starting to plough:

'All hail, Earth, mother of men!'

This is so obviously heathen that even today it almost dances off the page. Why retain such a reference to a female earth deity at a time when the Church was doing everything possible to suppress such things? There must have been some good reason why the Earth (and not the Virgin Mary) was still being addressed as the 'mother of men'. Probably the answer lies somewhere in what we already know about people's reluctance to abandon their old beliefs. The Land Remedy Charm was ancient and revered. It was vital that certain aspects were kept intact.

Next the spell-caster had to turn three times 'with the course of the sun,' and prostrate himself on the ground, while reciting various Christian formulae. Straight after that however, the instructions gallop off into pure folk magic: Let 'unknown seed be taken from beggars, and let twice as much be given to these as was taken from them.'

Now we might feel that taking seeds from beggars is about as low as one could possibly stoop, but this was not theft, because twice as much had to be given back in return. The important thing is that seeds were not purchased. This is curiously similar to traditional gardening lore, with certain plants said to thrive only if they are stolen or given away. Giving back double the amount of seed magically increases the land's fertility on the basis of 'Just as I give you double the amount of seed, so may the land produce double the weight of crops.'

Magically speaking, the seed and bread in this spell also work on the 'just as...so may' principle: just as the bread started out as seeds growing in the earth, then when they are returned to the earth, so earth's fertility comes full cycle once more and may increase.

In the next part of the spell, the landowner must gather his ploughing implements together and bore a hole in the beam of the plough. This shows his active involvement in the magical process, i.e. the charm was not simply performed on his behalf. Into the hole he places incense, fennel, hallowed soap and hallowed salt followed by the seed. Whether the salt and soap were consecrated by the local clergy or the spell-caster himself is not specified. No method for doing this is suggested, perhaps because it was so well known that nobody thought to mention it. This is a common – and frustrating -

problem. Much of the information we lack today is due to people assuming that everyone else knew what they meant!

The Land Remedy Charm is also reminiscent of the ceremony of blessing the plough which was held in Church on the first Monday after Twelfth Night in January. Although literary accounts of the ritual may not go back much further than the Middle Ages (Hutton 1996 :126) it is possible the idea of blessing agricultural tools is much older and even pre-Christian.

Ploughs were important agricultural implements and must have been capable of being magically protected or indeed cursed. In the Middle Ages, plough lights were kept burning in Churches, and early Church texts often mention lights in connection with heathen rituals. Although no candles are lights are mentioned in the Land Remedy Charm, it was performed at night and given its complex nature, it is very unlikely everyone was fumbling around in the dark.

In the next part of the charm the spell-caster declared:

'Erce, erce, erce, mother of Earth,

May the Almighty, the eternal Lord, grant you

Fields flourishing and bountiful,

Fruitful and sustaining...

The various types of harvests are then recited, finishing with:

'And all the harvests of the earth!'

Finally the spell-caster implores:

Grant him, O eternal Lord,

And his saints in Heaven that be,

That his farm be kept from every foe,

And guarded from each harmful thing

*Of witchcrafts (*lyblāca*) sown throughout the land.*

The word 'Erce' *could* have been a name for the earth goddess, perhaps a goddess of fertility, or even Nerthus (mentioned by Tacitus). Erring on the side of caution however, we cannot even be certain that Erce *was* a name; it might have been an exclamation, rather like the Latin *eheu* which is roughly the equivalent of the English 'Oh dear!'

What is most intriguing though is that the word was retained at all, since it suggests there was no simple equivalent that could be used instead. Possibly even the monk who copied out the text was not sure who or what Erce was.

The word does have some similarities with the Anglo-Saxon *erc* meaning an ark or chest (Bosworth 1838: 104). Perhaps a chest or box represented the womb of the Mother Earth in some way although without some further supporting evidence this idea is pure speculation.

Finally, the spell ends with instructions to make a hand sized loaf using many different types of cereal. Again this magically symbolised plenty and fertility and had to be kneaded with milk and holy water. Whether the holy water was taken (secretly or openly) from Church or gathered, in heathen tradition, as dew, probably depended on the religious inclinations of the spell-caster, priest or land-owner.

The baked bread was then laid under the first furrow with the following statement: .

> *'Full field of food for the race of man*
>
> *Brightly blooming, be you blessed,*
>
> *In the holy name of Him who shapes*
>
> *Heaven, and earth whereon we dwell.*
>
> *May God, who made these grounds, grant growing gifts*
>
> *That all our grain may come to use.'*

Although when read, the words seem to refer to the Christian God, when spoken aloud they could equally easily refer to a heathen deity. The Anglo-Saxon charms are full of ambiguity and riddles to trip the unwary!

Other Land Charms

There are other Land Charms and Field Remedies, of course. One features something called St Columbkille's Circle (Grendon 1909 :205) This was a sun-wheel shape with an outer border, inscribed with a knife on a meal stone – probably a grinding or quern stone. Again the magic focuses on protecting the land in which the seeds will grow.

Scratching the charm into the grinding stone would have magically protected the grains as they were made into flour. Knives were often used in healing charms, so this could have been a way of healing grains that might have been hexed.

The sunwheel is an ancient symbol that pre-dates Christianity by many centuries if not millennia. And the fact that it is simply scratched onto the meal stone suggest the inscription was not meant to be permanent.

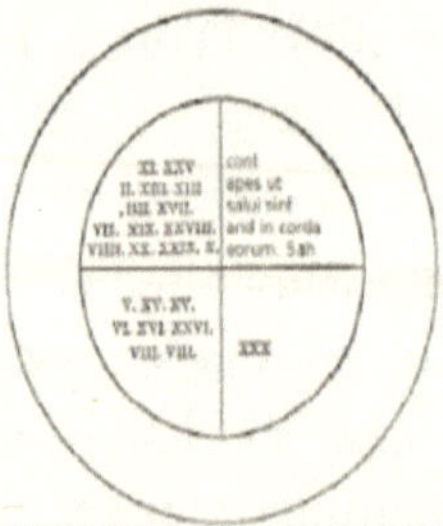

Certainly the charm is curious, just a few instructions and a diagram, without any spoken words. Three of the four quarters of the circle contain only Roman numerals. The wording is mostly Latin, and we can only hazard a guess at some of the words: *apes* might derive from aper/apri, Latin for a wild boar, raising images of the boar crest on the Sutton Hoo helmet. 'In corda eorum' could mean 'in their hearts,' (as it appears in the Book of Revelations, Ch. 17, v.17).

Even the diagram's name, 'St Columbkille's circle' is intriguing since Columbkille was a sixth century Irish missionary saint, who preached in Scotland. It seems unlikely therefore that he ever had any contact with the Anglo-Saxons. His name, Colum, means 'dove' in Gaelic, while *kille* means 'church'; taken together therefore Columbkille is generally thought to mean 'dove of the church.' He copied many manuscripts and wrote poems, and is thought to be one of the calligraphists who produced the beautiful Book of Kells.

So what can this charm tell us now? It has clearly been Christianised, featuring a saint, with close links with birds and writing. The most likely candidate for the original heathen deity has to be Woden. This is partly because as Odin in the Norse tradition, he discovered the runes which provides a natural link with Columbkille, the copier of manuscripts.

Secondly, Odin was associated with birds (especially his sacred ravens, Muninn and Huginn) while Columbkille's name links him with doves. Such associations could have made Columbkille a natural, Christian replacement for Woden, but only if the Anglo-Saxon Woden retained all the attributes of his Norse equivalent.

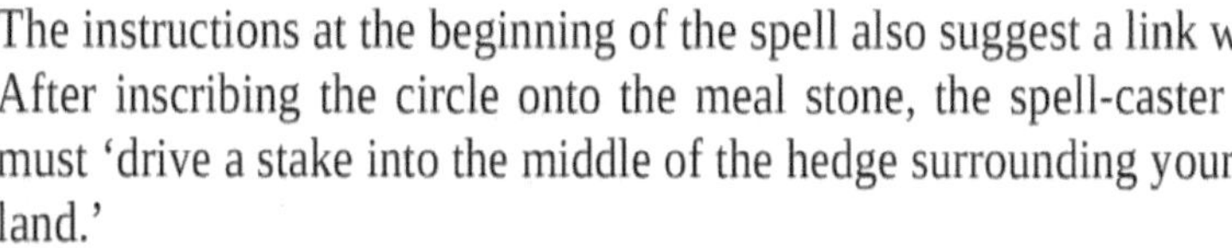

The instructions at the beginning of the spell also suggest a link w
After inscribing the circle onto the meal stone, the spell-caster
must 'drive a stake into the middle of the hedge surrounding your
land.'

Stakes and spears were Woden's sacred emblems. A buckle
plate from Kent (shown below) shows him almost naked,
wearing a horned helmet and holding two spears (Wilson 1992:116)

The Nine Herbs Charm

The Nine Herbs Charm is probably the most famous of the Anglo Saxon
charms and the only one to mention Woden by name. It occurs in the
Lacnunga, one of the Anglo-Saxon herbals as Charms number 79-82. Both
the Lacnunga and the Nine Herbs Charm are later names; nobody is quite
sure what they were originally called.

The Charm begins by addressing the herbs directly (Grendon 1909:191)

> *Remember, Mugwort, what you revealed,*
>
> *What you prepared at Regenmeld.*
>
> *Una, you are called, eldest of herbs.*
>
> *You avail against three and against thirty,*
>
> *You avail against poison and against infectious sickness,*
>
> *You avail against the loathsome fiend that wanders through the*
> *land.*
>
> *And you, Plantain, mother of herbs,*
>
> *Open from the east, mighty from within.*
>
> *Over you carts creaked, over you queens rode,*
>
> *Brides exclaimed over you, over you bulls gnashed their teeth.*
>
> *Yet all these you withstood and fought against:*
>
> *So may you poison and infectious sicknesses resist*
>
> *And the loathsome fiend that wanders through the land.*
>
> *Stime this herb is named; on stone it grew.*
>
> *It stands against poison, it combats pain.*
>
> *Fierce it is called, it fights against venom,*

It expels malicious [demons], it casts out venom.

This is the herb that fought against the snake,

This avails against venom, it avails against infectious illnesses,

It avails against the loathsome fiend that wanders through the land.

Fly now, Betonica, the less from the greater,

The greater from the less, until there be a remedy for both.

Remember, Camomile, what you revealed,

What you brought about at Alorford:

That he nevermore gave up the ghost because of ills infectious,

Since Camomile into a drug for him was made.

This is the herb called Wergulu.

The seal sent this over the ocean's ridge

To heal the horror of other poison.

These nine fought against nine poisons:

At first sight this all seems pretty straightforward. It is called the Nine Herbs Charm so it must address nine herbs. But is that really what happens? Mugwort is a herb, certainly, along with plantain, stime, betonica, camomile and wergulu. Una is more ambiguous. Two other herbs appear later, they are Fille and Finule (thought to be thyme and fennel). Unless we count Una as a herb, there are only eight.

Although Regenmeld is presented as an actual place or event, the word comprises the Anglo-Saxon words 'regen' meaning 'very' or 'most' as a prefix, and *meld* meaning discovery or evidence. Perhaps therefore the leech is reminding mugwort of the great evidence it has already provided (i.e. of its powers.) 'Alorford' (meaning ford of the alder tree - alders often grow near water) may well have been a real place, although its location and significance have long since been forgotten.

The next part of the charm reads like a narrative introduction:

A snake came sneaking, it slew a man.

Then Woden took nine glory twigs

And struck the serpent so that in nine parts it flew.

The *wyrm* played an important role in Anglo-Saxon magical thought and was applied to both dragons and serpents. Dragon legends are surprisingly persistent, with St George and the Dragon and the story Beowulf containing just two well known English examples. In Norse mythology it is Thor not Woden who battles repeatedly against the *miðgarðsormr* (Midgard serpent), a huge beast usually shown with its tail in its mouth.

Images of circular snake figures are widespread, and known by various other names, including the Greek *ourobouros* (meaning 'tail eating'). It features in cultures as far afield as India, Mexico, Egypt and the Graeco-Roman world. Although such imagery seems absent from Anglo-Saxon culture, there appears to be some evidence for it in this charm.

Think about what it tells us: Woden took nine glory twigs and sliced the dragon into nine parts, presumably one part for each of the *wuldortānas* or glory twigs, (although sometimes this is translated as a thunderbolt.) No-one is quite sure what a glory twig was; it's often suggested they were twigs inscribed with powerful runes, since *tān* was sometimes used to mean a twig used in casting lots.

However it can also describe a willow twig, and since willow was traditionally used in protective folk magic in England it is possible that *wuldortānas* were in fact taken from the willow tree. Unfortunately these are just theories, even if runes were inscribed on the twigs, we have no idea which ones were used.

The most interesting thing about this part of the charm however is that Woden used the nine twigs to cut the serpent into nine parts because if you make nine cuts (one for each of the nine glory twigs) on anything straight, you actually end up with *ten* pieces, not nine.

The charm however states that the serpent was cut into nine parts. It's tempting to think this was just a mistake, that the scribe meant eight parts, and that the number of parts didn't really matter. Or even that glory twigs in the hands of the gods could produce however many segments were required!

However, the Nine Herbs Charm repeatedly places emphasis not only on the number nine but also the number three. There are nine (3 times 3) herbs, nine accursed spirits, nine poisons, nine glory twigs, nine pieces of serpent and nine infections. The phrase 'against three and against thirty,' the three cardinal directions, the instructions to pronounce the incantation three times are obvious links with the number three and not nine, while there are six blisters (3 times 2).

So what sort of serpent was really being described in the charm? Because if Woden intended the snake to break into nine pieces or (which seems likely given that nine is a common number throughout) he should have used *eight* glory twigs. Unless....the serpent was actually a tail eating one. Then the nine glory twigs would indeed produce nine segments:

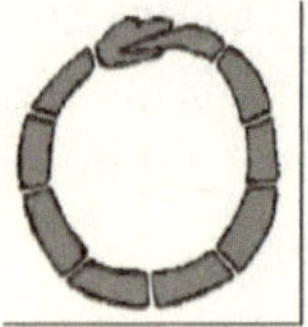

If this theory is correct, then the struggle between the serpent and Woden takes on the more cosmic nature of Thor and the Midgard Serpent. So what we have here in the Nine Herbs Charm could be the earliest surviving reference to an early, otherwise lost Anglo-Saxon version of the tail eating serpent.

The link between serpent (or dragon, or *wyrm*) and Woden also occurs in Norse legends. For example, in the Norse Gylfaginning (34), the All-Father (Odin) : 'sent the gods in order to get the children... And when they came to him, he threw the serpent into the deep sea which lies around all lands. And the serpent grew so that it lies in the middle of the ocean encircling all lands and bites on its own tail.' (Sturluson 1982: 27).

As we have already noted, it is uncertain whether or not Una was actually a herb in its own right. If not, then the only other option to make up the nine herbs is the apple, '... *There apple destroyed the serpent's poison: That it nevermore in house would dwell.'* Although most people might not think of apples as herbs, the word '*wyrt*' can mean not just a herb but a plant in a more general sense. Next we read:

> *These herbs the wise Lord created,*
>
> *Holy in heaven, while hanging [on the cross].*
>
> *He laid and placed them in the seven worlds,*
>
> *As a help for the poor and the rich alike.*

At first sight this seems to refer to the Crucifixion, until we realise the translator has added the words 'on the cross' which were not in the original.

In Norse mythology, according to the Hávamál, Odin hung for nine days and nights on the 'windswept Tree.' If we go back to the Nine Herbs Charm and remove the words in the brackets, we see that the 'Lord' could indeed be Woden, hanging on something that must have been so well known there was no need to explain.

This link with a particular aspect of Woden/Odin, that of discovering and claiming the runes could also support the theory that the glory twigs were indeed inscribed with runes. If true, it could drastically alter our perception of Anglo-Saxon religious and magical belief, particularly as regards divination.

The 'seven worlds' mentioned in the charm are something of a mystery, and this is the only example of a number not connected to the number three in the charm. Whether it was a later addition (or indeed an earlier one) is impossible to tell but certainly the number seven was not as popular with the Anglo-Saxons as it was with many other cultures.

The charm then continues with a list of all the problems that may be conquered, a vivid example of the magical threats bandied about in the magical world of the Anglo-Saxons:

> *It stands against pain, it fights against poison,*
>
> *It is potent against three and against thirty,*
>
> *Against a demon's hand, and against sudden guile,*
>
> *Against enchantment by vile creatures.*
>
> *Now these nine herbs avail against nine accursed spirits,*
>
> *Against nine poisons and against nine infectious ills,*
>
> *Against the red poison, against the running poison,*
>
> *Against the white poison, against the blue poison,*
>
> *Against the yellow poison, against the green poison,*
>
> *Against the black poison, against the blue poison,*
>
> *Against the brown poison, against the purple poison*

Apart from the difficulties of identifying plants in the Anglo-Saxon charms, it can also be difficult to identify colours precisely. Red for example, covers a wide range of shades from terracotta to crimson, while blue can vary from clear cobalt to deep indigo. It is not clear why poisons were listed according to colour. Possibly the spell-caster used items of various colours to enhance the dramatic impact.

Against worm-blister, against water-blister

Against thorn-blister, against thistle-blister,

Against ice-blister, against poison-blister,

If any poison come flying from the east, or any come from the north,

Or any come from the west upon the people.

Sometimes the poison flying from the east is translated as infection, perhaps because of what we know nowadays about airborne infectious diseases. In the original Anglo-Saxon, the word used was *attor*, meaning poison. The southern compass direction is missing, perhaps because the leech (or patient) faced this direction when the charm was performed.

Christ stood over poison of every kind.

I alone know [the use of] running water, and the nine serpents take heed [of it].

All pastures now may spring up with herbs,

The seas, all salt water, vanish,

When I blow this poison from you.

The main problem with translations is that a single line can have several very different versions. For example 'poison of every kind' can also be translated as 'ancient malevolent race.' As for blowing the poison, this could refer to sucking out the poison and then spitting it out, or even to the magical act of blowing upon a patient to exorcise him. This method was often used in ancient Greece and perhaps also by the Anglo Saxons.

Chapter Seventeen

Symbols, Words and other magical methods

A

ppealing to a higher power or superior spirit is a very ancient Indo-European magical technique. In the case of the Anglo-Saxon charms, which were transcribed by Christian monks, allusions to the original Pagan gods were usually (though not always) replaced by God, Christ, the Virgin Mary, the

Trinity, the Evangelists, one of the patriarchs, saints, prophets, or disciples.

However there remain several interesting examples where the person performing the spell appeals to what seem to be pagan powers. For example, the spell 'Against a swarm of bees' (Grendon 1909 Charm A4 :169) instructs 'take earth, with your right hand throw it under your right foot and say:

> *Lo earth is potent against every sort of creature,*
>
> *And against hatred and against forgetfulness,*
>
> *And against the mighty spell of man.*

Here it is earth that is 'potent' against every sort of creature, whereas in post-conversion England we might expect this to be God or the saints. Bees were important to the Anglo-Saxon rural economy, and losing a swarm threatened financial ruin for their owner. The ideal solution to any threatened desertion was to either prevent them swarming at all or convince them to set up a new hive elsewhere on the owner's land.

As we have already noted, appeals to earth in some shape or form are quite common in the Anglo-Saxon charms where it is addressed as 'Erce', Mother of Earth; 'Earth, Mother of Men' (Grendon 1909:173-7 A13) or 'May Earth remove you with all her might and main' (Grendon 1909:195 Charm B5). This suggests that although Earth was a heathen goddess, those in need still appealed to her with every hope of success.

In the first half of the spell the physical act of placing earth beneath the right foot is a physical link to the magical act of invoking the earth and its power. This is supported by the statement that 'earth is potent' which surely refers to some sort of earth deity. The intention is to counteract the spells of any rival magician who might be causing the bees to swarm.   Invoking the earth will magically 'ground' the bees by using the magical technique of like curing like (*similia similibus curantur*), another very old magical technique found in some shape or form almost all over the world.

The spell continues with instructions to throw gravel at the bees once they begin to swarm, while saying:

> *Alight, victory dames, sink to the ground!*
>
> *Never fly wild to the woodland!*
>
> *Be as mindful of my profit*
>
> *As is every man of food and home.*

In the original Anglo-Saxon text, the 'victory dames' are *sigewif*, one of several titles bestowed upon the Germanic Valkyries. Although it is highly unlikely the Valkyries were involved in the bees' activities, by flattering the bees, it was hoped to persuade them to stay.

This charm shows that Anglo-Saxon magic operated in much the same way as magic all over the world. In any type of magical work where one faces a hostile power, there are two basic choices, flattery or threat. Normally, the preferred option is flattery since nobody wants to face an angry spirit or demon if they can avoid it! Here appealing to the *sigewif* hopes to persuade by using flattery, rather like addressing a humble police constable as 'inspector.'

Addressing an entity as '*sigewif*' is not confined to bees; I have even known people successfully use it to deal with boisterous house brownies! Also the technique of flattery is often used in healing rather than the more dangerous options of physically harming the patient in order to persuade the sickness demon to leave.

Of course, a very powerful spell-caster (or at least one who wanted to appear that way) might be bold enough to start off with threats instead. We see this too, in the Anglo Saxon Charms, with the simple Christianised command, '*fuge diabolus, Christus te sequitur*'(Grendon 1909:187 Charm A23). This may have replaced an earlier, now lost, heathen threat formula.

As a middle option, spell-casters simply listed their own powers – a magical CV or advertisement designed to impress the victim and intimidate the opposition. Again, this practice was standard throughout Indo-European magic.

Names and Words of Power

Names and words of power are an important aspect of all spell work and have been a popular component in charms since ancient times. Magically speaking, if you name something, you claim authority over it, which makes it particularly useful in healing spells.

In healing charms especially, it was important the patient trusted whoever was performing the spell on his behalf to exercise power by virtue of the names and words he used. In that sense, when the patient is named she temporarily gives up all control and entrusts herself entirely to the magician or leech.

There are only a handful of naming examples in the Anglo-Saxon Charms. This could either mean that the Anglo-Saxons did not regard naming as particularly important or that naming the patient (and sometimes also his father) was so commonplace that it was taken as a given. Possibly the inclusion of the father's name was to make sure there was no confusion, rather like using someone's surname nowadays.

Curiously, the *precise* names of the entities responsible are rarely stated. Instead they are referred to generically as elves, dwarves, night visitors etc. This is curious in view of the magical theory that naming something gives one power over it. However, by the time the Anglo-Saxon Charms were written down, they had been Christianised, and therefore more likely to name the saint or angel being invoked to help than the disease demon being confronted.

Possibly Christian scribes deliberately avoided naming what they believed were heathen demons because they feared that naming something could make it materialise. This would then be similar to the Egyptian idea of obliterating all trace of something one wished to destroy, and the rise of the 'he-who-shall-not-be-named' formulae. Generally speaking Christians blamed the Devil for most illnesses, for example, referring to insanity as 'devil sickness'. We cannot be certain exactly who – or what – was blamed by the heathen Anglo-Saxons.

There are also words of power in the Charms but these have often been overlooked and even mistaken for gibberish (Grendon 1909:105, 114). In fact they are nothing of the sort. Although a few *may* have become unintelligible with the passage of time, I suspect others may be disguises. If we name something in a way that only we can understand then magically we are concealing its power while maintaining our own. This technique is particularly useful when dealing with another, hostile magician.

One such spell, to cure people and animals of worms begins with the instruction that it should be sung into a man's right ear, or a woman's left one (Grendon 1909:169 Charm A5). The actual charm reads:

> *Gonomil, orgomil, marbumil,*
>
> *Marbsairamum tofeð tengo,*
>
> *Docuillo biran cuiðær,*
>
> *Cæfmiil scuiht cuillo scuiht*

Cuib duill marbsiramum.

Obviously we have no idea what it means. Possibly the original words were passed down orally, becoming corrupted by the time it was written down. Or perhaps the scribe deliberately misrepresented them. And while some will claim this type of spell was a nonsense designed just to impress, there is no evidence for that, either!

Often it is not even clear what language is being used. For example, a charm 'Against Thefts' (Grendon 1909:169 Charm A6) reads:

Luben luben biga.

Efið efið niga

Fel ceid fel,

Delf cymer fel

Orcgaei ceufor dar

Giug farig fidig

Delou delupih

At first sight, it looks like Anglo-Saxon, although very few words are recognisable apart from *fel* (skin); *biga* (corner) and *delf* (meaning digging). The driving rhythm of the words remains strong however, suggesting it was an important part of ensuring the spell reached its destination.

Occasionally we encounter names from traditions normally far removed from Anglo-Saxon culture. Such exotic words may well have been considered powerful. For example, in a charm against Ague, we encounter Leleloth and Tiecon, two Arabian deities, amidst all the Paternosters and Masses (Grendon 1909:183 Charm A18). The careful instructions for herb preparation suggest the charm's heathen origins.

Elsewhere, in a charm to heal a horse's sprain, the Babylonian king Naborredus is invoked (Grendon 1909:183 Charm A19). Also Deus, Emanuel, and Adonai (the latter used particularly for dealing with 'evil spirits') also occur regularly along with words in Latin, Greek, Hebrew, Gaelic, and others.

Magic Symbols

Magic symbols occur regularly in the Charms. These include Alpha and Omega (sometimes written out in full, or as A and Ω or even as *alpha et o*).

These were usually used healing spells, a tradition practised by Greek physicians since ancient times. Although Alpha and Omega are associated with Christ, they are of course the first and last letters of the Greek Alphabet. Possibly Anglo Saxon magic absorbed and made use of other traditions alongside its own or perhaps Christian clerics simply inserted these letters into the charms to replace other, heathen symbols, when they copied them out.

Other symbols encountered in the charms include strings of letters, dots and crosses. For example, there is a charm 'Concerning Magic Writings' (Grendon 1909: 203 Charm D7) which includes a formula to ensure that influential people will always be well disposed towards the bearer:

XX. h. d. e. o. e. o. o. o. e. e. e. laf. d. R. U. fi.ð . f . p. A. x. Box. Nux. In nomine patris Rex. M . p . x . XIX . xls . xli. ih. + Deo. eo. deo. deeo . lafdruel. bepax. box . nux . bu . In nomine patris rex mariæ . Jesus Christus dominus meus . Jesus + . Eonfra . senioribus . H . hrinlur . her . letus contra me . hee . larrhibus excitatio pacis inter virum and mulierem A. B. and alfa tibi reddit uota fructu leta . lita . tota . tauta . uel tellus et ade uirescit

With this amount of much writing, it is likely this charm required the co-operation of a priest or someone in holy Orders. Whether the Latin phrases were tacked onto the end of a line of heathen sigils, we will probably never know. What this type of charm tells us however, is that writing quickly became imbued with a power of its own.

The following charm, to protect against being hexed, could have been written out by almost anyone since it involves minimal copying (Grendon 1909:204 Charm A19) :

<pre>
    +   o
</pre>

+ A + + O + Y + ipByM + + + + + : BeroNNIKNETTANI

In a charm against Ague, the patient is told to carry the following inscription 'on his left breast', but only for as long as he is out of doors, on no account must it be carried indoors (Grendon 1909:203 Charm D9).

⋈MMRMþ. Nandþ TX ⋈ MREwNandþTX.

This shows the Anglo-Saxon belief that being indoors was magically quite different from being outside. Such belief also occurs in literature, where Bede recounts how Augustine first landed in England in 597CE, and set out to visit Æthelbert, the Saxon King of Kent. Instead of inviting Augustine into his home, the king took the unusual precaution of setting up camp on an island, 'For he had taken precaution that they should not come to him in any house, lest, according to an ancient superstition, if they practiced any magical arts they might impose upon him, and so get the better of him.' (Bede EHEN I:25.)

Although it is tempting to view Æthelbert as overly superstitious and paranoid, we must remember this is only Bede's view of what was going on. For all we know it may have been customary to meet strangers out in the open and not invite them indoors until one could be certain of their intentions.

Alternatively perhaps the Anglo-Saxons believed that magic was less likely to affect them out of doors. In that case, we have to wonder how they believed such magic could have been performed, perhaps by secretly leaving a cursed object in the home? At the moment we can only speculate. However, if people really felt safer out of doors, this would have important implications for rural communities where so much of the daily work was done out in the fields, gardens and woodland. Possibly people sensed a different atmosphere indoors, something only conducive to certain types of magic.

The same charm continues with instructions to silently put on a second piece of writing:

HAMMANyᵒEL . BPONICe . NOYᵒewTAyᵒEPG.

Several Anglo Saxon Charms stress the importance of silence while the ritual is performed. This is very similar to the folk tradition of not speaking while gathering nettles (popularly known as 'silent nettles.')

There is a similar example in a charm to identify a thief (Grendon 1909: 207 Charm D12). This involved copying out the charm in silence and placing it in the heel of one's left shoe. Placing plants and charms in the shoe has been a very persistent folk tradition, practised right up into Victorian times. It has the advantage of privacy, because only the wearer knows it is there. The charm itself did not require real literacy, and was set out thus:

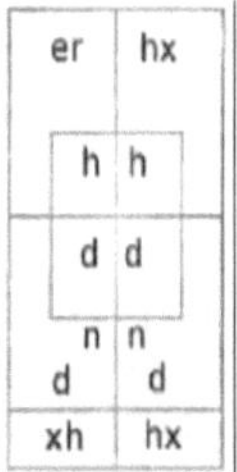

What this symbolised is anyone's guess. It's tempting to view it as a mirror image, but look carefully and you will see this does not apply to the *er – hx* letters at the top.

Not all charms were so secretive. One, for dealing with nosebleeds, had to be written directly on the patient's forehead: (Grendon 1909: 211 E7)

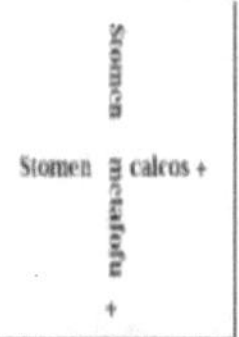

Magically this could work by transferring the power of the inscription directly to the patient *via* the skin, although other examples could transfer to a magical tool, scrap of paper or even a herbal potion. Interestingly, although the runic letters, ð and þ appear in some charms, they only appear as letters of the alphabet and not as symbols. Evidence for the magical use of runes is often cited from the Norse tradition's Poetic Edda, (Sigrdrifumól, 14-20) but of course this is not an Anglo-Saxon text, although they may have had some similar practices. It is possible (although not provable) that all runes were replaced by the mark of the cross.

Other magical methods

Modern readers are often shocked that the Anglo-Saxon Charms often recommend subjecting sick patients to physical violence such as scourging. In fairness, such methods are found in many other periods and cultures too. The magical thinking behind it was that a demon or entity had brought the sickness to the patient (animal or human). So if the entity could be made uncomfortable enough, it would no longer want to occupy the patient's body and would leave.

This method is still the basis of many modern exorcisms. Of course, the downside is that if the patient doesn't recover, or still shows symptoms of 'possession' then the cruelty is increased and the patient may even die as a result. We have no idea whether or how often this happened in Anglo-Saxon England, but it is quite possible. It does still happen sometimes today, even in the West.

A less violent method of driving out evil spirits was to use the smoke of burning herbs, especially smearwort (*Aristolochia rotunda*) which was sometimes burned with frankincense. This was probably preferable to being made to eat or drink revolting things such as cakes containing the dung of a white dog,(Grendon 1909:211 Charm E11) or drinking dog's vomit (*ibid:117*)!

Dung seems to played an important role in Anglo Saxon magic. For example, anyone wishing the ability to cure abdominal pains for the next twelve months first had to catch a dung beetle and its excrement in both hands then wave it around before throwing it away backwards and without looking at it (Grendon 1909:199 Charm C2).

Human saliva is another widely used remedy in folk medicine all over the world, especially for helping sores to heal. When I was young I was taught that spittle's natural antiseptic properties could be used magically for many types of healing, and not just for skin diseases. The Anglo Saxons also used it in a charm to cure pain in the Limbs, advising, 'Sing nine times the following charm thereon, and spit your spittle on [the place affected]' (Grendon 1909:185 Charm A20).

Spittle is also recommended in an Anglo-Saxon charm for curing scabies (Grendon 1909 :197 Charm C1). First many herbs including elecampane, viper's bugloss and bishop's wort had to be mixed together with goose-grease and old soap. Then the patient waited until night before applying the mixture to her body. Next she had to scratch her neck until it bled (not difficult with a condition like scabies), washing the blood into running water and spitting three times, all in absolute silence.

The use of running water shows the charm was performed out of doors so that when the patient declared, 'Take this evil [thing] and move away with it,' the scabies was magically transferred into the water and removed both from the patient and her community. Finally, she had to return home by an open road, again in complete silence.

While saliva and even dung, can be easily obtained, the same cannot be said of applying grated or burned human skull bone to the skin (Grendon

1909:123). Although it sounds too fantastic to be true, it is corroborated to some extent in Burchard, (Paragraph 164A) where a burned skull was used to make a 'tonic drink.'

This strongly suggests the Anglo-Saxons must have brought this particular type of magic with them from their Germanic homelands. However we must be careful not to jump to the conclusion that this somehow 'proves' that they brought everything else mentioned in Burchard with them too!

Spells and the body

Many Anglo-Saxon charms are instructed to be sung or written on certain parts of the body, especially on the left hand side although occasionally they are repeated elsewhere and, as we have already seen, may even be written across the face.

Spells must sometimes be said close to certain parts of the body. For example, a charm against Erysipelas,(Grendon 1909:173 Charm A11) must be sung on top of the man's head but into the horse's left ear. The famous charm 'Against a dwarf'(Grendon 1909: 168 Charm A2) was directed to be sung first into the left ear, then into the right, and then over the head. After that it had to be written on communion wafers and hung around the patient's neck for three days.

The use of writing and communion wafers indicates that people in holy orders were regularly persuaded to take part in such charms.

The right side of the body (usually the ear) was not as popular as the left in the Anglo-Saxon Charms, although curiously it is mentioned in an old Danish exorcism charm, 'I lay me on my right side, so shall I sleep with Lady Freya. Get out, Ragirist! come in, Mary, with Jesus Christ!' (Grimm 1842: Vol 3:506, liii) Clearly this charm has been only partially Christianised, since Freya is mentioned in the same breath as Jesus and Mary. It is therefore possible – though not provable – that the Anglo-Saxons also associated sleeping on the right side with Freya.

While the left ear was the most popular place for charm singing, the left shoe was popular for hiding written charms and herbs. This tradition continued in English folk magic right into the nineteenth century. Written charms could also be inscribed on or carried near the arm, forehead, head, tongue, breast, limbs, or on or near the wound or painful part of the body.

Charms could also be sung against objects. For example, a charm to cure diarrhoea had to be sung on a soft boiled egg nine times for three days although it is not specified whether this must be the *same* egg. (Grendon 1909 :171 Charm A8) When charms involved horses, the spell was sometimes sung on a barley loaf which the animal was then given to eat. If a horse had been stolen, the charm could be sung on its fetters, bridle, or footprints. Spells were even sung on the four sides of a house!

Special times of day

The Anglo-Saxon charms often specify a particular time for performing magic. Usually this was night time, although in the absence of clocks, the exact part of the night could be described as evening, after sunset, 'at night before going to bed' or before daybreak. In the case of healing spells, the magical intention may have been to harness the power of the disappearing light (or darkness) to make the illness vanish too. Occasionally spells must be performed during the day 'ere the setting of the sun' (all from Grendon 1909:119).

Sometimes certain moon- phases are specified. These can be a precise date from the first appearance of the new moon, or more general such as a waxing or waning moon in a particular season of the year. When the exact age of the moon is specified, it is often a product of multiplying by five. This is interesting because when numbers appear in the Charms, they are almost always products of the number three (i.e. six, nine or twelve.)

Sometimes spells had to be performed before the moon appeared in the sky, either after sunset or before moonrise. Again indicates that certain times were thought to be more powerful than others. The fact that the moonphases and times of day varied suggests they believed that certain times and dates etc., had power over particular types of problems.

Occasionally several different times of day appear within a single charm showing that magic was no 'quick fix' but could require extensive effort. For example, in the Leechbook of Bald, a charm 'For Elf disease' (Grendon 1909:p191) should begin on Thursday evening 'when the sun is set.' Thursday was sacred to Thunor, and although the spoken parts of the charm have been highly Christianised, the actions remain noticeably heathen. This is a very typical feature of the Anglo-Saxon charms: heathen actions and Christian words.

This charm against Elf disease is worth examining in greater detail. The leech or spell caster must go to an elecampane plant, singing a benedicite, paternoster and litany, which are probably Christian substitutions for heathen herb-gathering formulae, and 'stick your knife into the herb.' The knife was left in place overnight until daybreak, when 'day and night divide.'

Next the leech had to go to church and 'cross yourself and commend yourself to God,' which is interesting in view of the fact that many Church authors condemned such practices. Presumably there was a certain amount of guilt or unease, best shown in the strange comment 'though something of a fearful kind.... should come upon you.'

Once this had been accomplished, the leech had to return in silence to the herb with the knife still sticking out of it. After singing yet another Benedicite, Paternoster and litany he could dig up the herb but was not allowed to remove the knife while doing so, which must have been a pretty messy business all around. He then had to go back to the church and somehow shove the plant with its knife under the altar, leaving it there until the sun had risen. This could hardly have taken more than a few minutes, since he had to start digging the herb just after daybreak anyway.

Next the herb had to be made up into a drink with bishop's wort and lichen from a crucifix, boiled three times in milk and have water added to it three times. Then the Paternoster and litany were sung again, together with a Gloria. The whole was then marked with a cross on four sides. How this was done is not clear from the text, possibly the container was marked, or it was set on the floor and the crosses marked around it.

This charm clearly shows the complicated relationship between its heathen and Christianised aspects. The Church, although condemning magic, was nevertheless deeply involved in it – or at least some of the clergy must have been. And the fact that the Charms were preserved at all shows how persistently they were practised.

The 'Just as...so may' formula

Like many other cultures, the Anglo-Saxons made extensive use of the 'just as... so may' formula. This links the power of a physical act to the desired magical result. So you might have something like, 'Just as I burn this piece of wood, so may the fever be burned out of the patient.'

However whereas heathen comparisons tend to focus on the natural world and its phenomena (as in the piece of wood) Christianised versions tended to draw their comparisons from the Bible and stories of the saints. Christians were not really interested what plants symbolised because they believed everything – life, death etc. was controlled by their God. The upshot of course was that eventually the Church taught that all human pain and suffering was caused by evil, and sent by God both as a punishment and as a test of faith.

Although it was sometimes permitted to eat healing plants or lay them on wounds, adding a few enchantments or spells was firmly forbidden especially by the Carthusian and Cistercian orders, both founded in the eleventh century. Seeking miracles from shrines however was usually encouraged by Church authorities as grateful supplicants made offerings for their cures.

Of course charm formulae can be very subtle. Two charms intended to recover stolen cattle use the same formula, 'The Jews crucified Christ, they did the worst of deeds to him; they hid what they could not hide, so may this deed never be hidden.' (Grendon 1909:185 Charms A21 and A22) In other words, the thief's identity would be known and the cattle recovered. Here the 'Just as.... so may' formula is closely linked to the magical method of *similia similibus curantur* (like curing like) and is particularly noticeable in those charms that have been heavily Christianised.

In the less Christianised charms however, such comparisons are drawn from natural phenomena. Sometimes both heathen and Christianised comparisons exist side-by-side in the same charm. For example, in another charm to find lost cattle, the introduction states 'May nothing I own be stolen or hidden any more than Herod could steal or hide our Lord.'(Grendon 1909: 181 Charm A16) Yet the active part of the charm goes on to invoke the mysterious 'Garmund, servitor of God'.

Garmund is something of a puzzle. His name is made up of the Anglo Saxon words *gar-* meaning a spear or weapon and *mund* meaning protection. One possibility is that Garmund was an epithet for Woden, since the spear was one of his attributes. His presence in the Charm suggests a heathen entity who had been turned into a servant of God so that he could remain the power behind the charm.

Whoever Garmund really was, it is impossible to read the invocation without being moved by its wonderful natural imagery and driving rhythm.

Garmund, servitor of God,

Find those kine and fetch those kine,

And have those kine and hold those kine

And bring home those kine

That he never may have land to lead them to,

Nor fields to fetch them to,

Nor houses to confine them in.

Should any man so act, may he thereby never prosper!

Within three days his powers I'll know,

His skill and his protecting crafts!

May he be quite destroyed as fire destroyeth wood,

As bramble or as thistle injures thigh,

He who may be planning to bear away these cattle

Or purposing to drive away these kine.

Looking more closely at this charm we see how Garmund was invoked to protect against theft by magical and physical means and any would-be thief was cursed *in advance* of the actual act. We also see clear heathen examples of nature based comparisons:

May he be quite destroyed as fire destroyeth wood,

As bramble or as thistle injures thigh

Charms against theft are particularly interesting because they give us some idea how the Anglo-Saxons believed that magic worked. For example, in another charm he spell-caster is instructed to sing the charm on the stolen horse's fetters or bridle, or on the footprints of stolen cattle (who obviously possess neither fetters nor bridle.) (Grendon 1909 :180)

This shows how things that were owned, worn or made by the missing animal were believed to be imbued with its magnetism. In the case of the footprints, the method is to pour wax on them, as a way of magically 'fixing ' them. Here the magical thinking is that just as the wax would quickly cool and set, so magically the cattle would also 'set' and be unable to move and further. This would probably work best with prints made as the animals were leaving or being lead away.

By the same token, using candles in charms to recover stolen goods would throw both physical and magical light upon both the missing items and the thief.

The role of Water

Heathen magic seems to have placed great stored in the power of running water. This, along with well and water worship and vigils at wells, seems to have been very common amongst the Germanic peoples both in England and on the continent. Such practices were repeatedly denounced in the decrees of the Church Councils and the various penitentials.

In Anglo-Saxon magical belief, every river and stream was home to a spirit to whom sacrificial offerings were made in order to propitiate them. Obviously this belief was not unique to the Anglo-Saxons and is found right across pre-Christian Europe. Also although many healing well and springs still exist in the English countryside, this did not all suddenly appear in the fifth or sixth centuries. Many of them may date back to primeval times.

Certainly such beliefs in the power of water were so entrenched that the early Church found it nearly impossible to eradicate them. Eventually the best option was to assimilate or Christianise most of them. Yet even though water deities were replaced by saints, the problem persisted, and in the twenty-sixth canon of St. Anselm (early twelfth century) we read, 'Let no one attribute reverence or sanctity to a fountain, without the Bishop's authority.' (Bourne 1725:66-67) Possibly it was more a question of power than theology. Provided the Church authorised and controlled it, a practice could be tolerated. Freelance 'magic' or religious ritual however, was condemned.

Although baptism is nowadays presented as a wholly Christian practice, the heathen Anglo Saxons also dipped newborn babies into running water. Christianising this ritual was easy, and the original version would soon have been forgotten.

Likewise running water was often sprinkled on warriors about to enter battle, because Woden had promised, 'If I pour water on the young warrior, he will not fall, even in battle; he will not be slain by the sword' (Gummere 1892: 393). So whenever charms specify holy water it seem likely that either dew or running water was used in the pre-Christian version (Chantepie 1902:128).

Traditionally, Germanic magical tradition held that the best healing water was drawn before sunrise, downstream and in silence. Water gathered in this way was supposed to remain fresh, restore youth, heal skin complaints and would make young cattle strong. Centuries later, women were still gathering dew (especially in May) in the belief that it gave them a beautiful complexion.

The necessity for silence is quite common in Anglo-Saxon magic, and is quite different from much of today's magical practice with its accompanying chants and rhymes. At first it seems curious, but perhaps it was intended to preserve secrecy and enhance concentration. It could also give the person performing the spell the benefit of surprise. This could certainly apply to charms intended to avert curses.

Another explanation – given the Church's hostility to heathen rituals - is that it had once been traditional to utter certain charms while herb gathering. As the conversion of England gathered pace, it was perhaps felt more prudent to be silent. Against this argument, however, is the fact that not all spells require silence, while many were Christianised by saying prayers or Christian formula while collecting or working with herbs.

Magic lines

There is some evidence that the Anglo-Saxons used 'magic lines' to draw directly around the disease or the patient. A charm against erisypelas reads: 'Take a green stick and have the man sit in the middle of the floor of the house, and make a stroke around him, and say, *'O pars et o rlllla pars et pars iniopia est alfa et o initium.* (Grendon 1909 :173 Charm A12)

Since the type of tree is not specified, the 'green stick' was probably a length of wood cut from any living tree and we must assume its power lay solely in the fact that it was green, i.e. full of sap. The charm does not stipulate that the 'stroke around him' was a circle, although it seems likely otherwise there would have been no need to place the man in the middle of the floor.

Magic lines could also be drawn with the hand around a wound or sore. Of course drawing a physical line around rashes and swellings has practical benefits too since it enables us to see whether it is getting worse or the infection is spreading.

In a charm to heal a strange swelling, the leech is instructed to sing the Paternoster three times on the little finger. This is interesting since we would expect the leechfinger (next to the little finger) to be used instead. While tracing around the swelling, the formula *'Fuge diabolus, Christus te sequitur.*

Quando natus est Christus, fugit dolor' had to be recited.   (Grendon 1909: 187 Charm A23) Both the paternoster and the *Fuge diabolus* were then repeated a further three times. This again shows a combination of Christian invocations and heathen actions.

The commonest numbers in Anglo-Saxon magic seem to have been focused on the number three, i.e. three, six, nine and twelve. Rituals often had to be repeated three or nine times or on that number of successive days. Sometimes the charms call for three or nine specific ingredients, e.g. leaves, herbs, nails etc. Masses, paternosters etc have to be repeated three or nine times. Clearly it would not have been difficult to shift the importance of three (and three related numbers) to the Trinity.   Although the number seven is popular in many traditions including Indo European folklore, it rarely appears in Anglo-Saxon charms.

Sometimes despite half-hearted attempts at Christianisation, the charms remain so far outside mainstream Church practice that you wonder what on earth the monks who transcribed them must have thought. For example, a charm 'For Delayed Birth'(Grendon 1909:207 Charm E1), intended to help a woman carry her child full term directs her to go to the 'grave of a wise man,' which she must step over three times.

Presumably the magical thinking behind this was that the pregnancy was being affected by an evil spirit which would then be transferred to the corpse. Having been a 'wise man' in life, the dead man would probably have known how to deal with it!

The next part of the charm was performed at bedtime, when the woman had to say to her husband:

Up I go, over you I step,

With a live child not with a dying one,

With a full-born child, not with a dead one.

Having transferred the disease demon into the grave, it seems likely now that the husband was allowing some of his own life force to pass into – and thereby strengthen – the child. Human nature being what it is, he was hardly likely to lie still and allow any disease-demon to pass into him, no matter how much his wife pleaded. Obviously the Church would have condemned this kind of magical work. The fact that it persisted nonetheless may explain why the Church's attitude eventually hardened towards magic. What it could not control, it had to eradicate.

Chapter Eighteen

Anglo-Saxon Magical Thinking

E

xamining some more charms line by line can tell us a great deal about how the Anglo-Saxons used and regarded magic. Although there are three main surviving texts, the *Lacnunga, The Leechbook of Bald* and *the Old English Herbarium*, along with a variety of other manuscripts, this must be a tiny percentage of the original magical tradition.

For example, the *Wiþ Wennum*, is a charm against a wen or cyst. The written version dates from the late eleventh century, although the oral original may be centuries older (Fry, 1971, p249). The basic translation (Grendon 1909 :167 Charm A3) is as follows:

> *Wen, Wen, Wen-chicken,*   *(1)*
>
> *Here you shall not build, nor have any dwelling,*
>
> *but you shall go north hence to the nearby fortress,*
>
> *where you wretched have a brother.*
>
> *He shall lay a leaf on your head. (5)*
>
> *Under the wolf's foot, under the eagle's feather,*
>
> *under the eagle's claw, ever may you fade away.*
>
> *May you shrink as coal on a hearth,*
>
> *may you shrivel as dung on a wall,*
>
> *and may you fade away as water in pail. (10)*
>
> *May you become as little as a linseed-grain,*
>
> *much less than a hand-worm's hipbone,*
>
> *and may you become so little that you become nothing.*

There are many things this text cannot tell us, such as the gestures used, ingredients, preparations or ritual objects etc., although some can be inferred from the text. First however, we must examine how the charm is laid out, and its structure. Briefly these are as follows:

Line 1 addresses the object of the charm, while lines 2 – 4 firmly tell it what it must do. Lines 5 – 7 include an interesting description of ritual medicine, showing the process used to make sickness disappear.

Lines 8 – 13 include a series of commands to reduce the wen until it becomes nothing at all. These use a version of the 'Just as.... so may' formula with similes, e.g. 'as little as a linseed grain.' If we look at each part in more detail, the structure and intention becomes clearer.

Now we shall look at each section in some more detail:

Line 1 – the object of the charm

Addressing the wen directly, suggests it was believed to be sentient, and could both listen and obey. The term 'Wen-chicken' could refer to the egg-like swelling, although it could also mean the spirit or force responsible for 'laying' the wen.

Alternatively the word 'chicken' may be used as an affectionate diminuitive, rather like calling a strapping six foot teenager 'son,' or 'little man.' In the original, the word is written 'Wennchichenne' and in German the 'chen' suffix denotes a diminuitive, for example *hund* (dog) becomes *hundchen*, (little dog or doggie). Perhaps the magical reasoning was that by trivialising the wen the leech was demonstrating his power over it. Lines 8 – 13 show this more clearly.

Lines 2- 4 narrative

Anglo Saxon charms often use various types of narration to show how something similar was dealt with in the past and implying that the same result will be achieved with the present charm. This charm uses something called a 'narrative prohibition' which sets out exactly what the wen is forbidden from doing: 'You shall not build, nor have any dwelling....' etc. Thus the person casting the spell asserts authority by a series of prohibitions, rather like modern signs stating 'Do not walk on the grass. Do not leave litter, etc.'

Lines 5 – 7 - Description of ritual medicine

Although we do not know what sort of ritual gestures, tools or talismans were used in performing this charm, lines 5 – 7 provide some useful clues. Possibly the appropriate actions accompanied each line. Firstly we read, 'He shall lay a leaf on your head.' The type of leaf is not specified nor whether it is fresh or dried. However we can assume it was large enough to hold the items that are listed afterwards, since even a shrivelled wolf's paw is fairly sizeable. Traditionally, butterbur leaves were traditionally popular for wrapping pats of butter but others would do. One of my aunts always made 'baskets' out of a variety of leaves whenever we went blackberry picking.

Lines 6 – 7 specify the items to be placed on the leaf: a wolf's foot, an eagle's feather and an eagle's claw. These may have formed part of a magician's ritual toolkit or they may have been specially collected for this spell. Although eagles and wolves would have been more common than they are now in northern Europe, it is also possible that ordinary objects were given fanciful names to make them appear more impressive. This was quite a common practice in magical recipes in the ancient Greco-Roman world and perhaps the Anglo-Saxons followed suit (Ogden 2009 :168).

Another possibility is that these items were intended to be used only as amulets, and it was enough just to place them on the patient for a short time while the spell was performed. Possibly the eagle's feather and claw were used to stroke or even scratch the wen which would be a form of magical attack. Wolves and eagles can both be fierce predators.

Certainly the eagle was significant for early Christians, which might explain why these items were retained when the charm was later transcribed. According to Bede, in his life of St Cuthbert, (Chapter 12) the saint described the eagle as 'our handmaid.'

Lines 8 – 13 the 'reducing' commands

In order to magically rid oneself of something there are two basic choices, either command it to depart immediately, or make it shrink in stages. The latter method seems to have been favoured by the Anglo-Saxons and there are a number of charms showing how it could be done.

In this charm we see the shrinking process compared to a series of vivid images designed to make visualisation – a very important part of magic – much easier for both the person performing the spell and the patient. Without effective visualisation, any charm is little more than a poetry recitation!

Yet if we look more closely we see there is more to these lines than simple visual images. Each relates to one of the four elements, Fire, Air, Water and Earth. For fire the command is to '*shrink as coal on a hearth*'; for air it is, '*shrivel as dung on a wall*' (bearing in mind that in the right conditions dung will dry out completely and scatter in the wind); for water there is '*fade away as water in pail,*' while earth is rendered as the linseed grain.

The hand-worm (*handwurmes*) was probably the tiny organism responsible for the wen. In stages therefore, using vivid images and the power of the four elements, the wen was reduced to something so tiny it was invisible to the human eye and thence to consigned to oblivion.

Counting Out

Another form of Anglo-Saxon magical healing uses the 'counting out method.' This is very similar to 'Ten Green Bottles' song we learned as children, a type of rhyme that has existed for centuries in many Germanic countries (Bolton 1888:45ff). A good Anglo-Saxon example appears in the charm *Wiþ Cyrnel* ('For a Kernel') which is a swelling, lump, or enlarged gland. (Grendon 1909:171 Charm A9)

Nine were Noththe's sisters,

Then the nine came to be VIII

And the VIII to VII

And the VII to VI

And the VI to V

And the V to IV

And the IV to III

And the III to II

And the II to I

And the I to nothing.

Although we have to be wary of creating links where none exist, this style of charm has persisted even into the late nineteenth and early twentieth century. In Cornwall it was used to treat 'tetter' (ringworm):

Tetter, tetter, thou hast nine brothers.

God bless the flesh and preserve the bone;

Perish, thou tetter, and be thou gone.

In the name, &c.

Tetter, tetter, thou hast eight brothers.

God bless the flesh and preserve the bone;

Perish, thou tetter, and be thou gone. In the name, &c...

(Hunt 1865 :414)

The charm continues down to nought. Although clearly Christianised, nevertheless it has preserved the 'reducing' element, and like the Anglo-Saxon charm, it begins with the magical number nine.

However, Cornwall is normally considered part of the Celtic fringe rather than belonging to the Anglo Saxon heartland. Possible explanations are that the charm was taken into Cornwall from nearby Wessex (the land of the West Saxons) or even that the Saxons adopted the charm from their Celtic neighbours, since similar charms turn up in Brittany (Conrad 1983, 104)

The Anglo-Saxon *Wiþ Cyrnel* charm was completed by singing the Benedicite nine times, a rather obvious attempt to Christianise something that was otherwise quite heathen. Although neither Noththe nor his/her sisters have been conclusively identified, the Anglo-Saxon word *noð* was sometimes used as a name ending, when it meant daring, while *nið* was a prefix meaning wicked or evil and *niðer* meant downward. Any or all of these meanings could be behind the original function of Noththe's sisters in making the kernel disappear.

Reducing charms were not only used on various types of swellings, but also on conditions like ringworm which spread throughout the body. It seems likely – although we cannot prove – that the same method could be used for reducing other things such as plague, perhaps reducing the number of cases until the epidemic was over.

The same method could also lend itself to countering spells intended to reduce fertility or make love disappear between two people. It could even have been used to reduce all manner of excesses from a bad temper to heavy snoring! We may not have written evidence for this, since the surviving literature must be only a fraction of what originally existed, but it remains a distinct possibility.

Using Intimidation in Magic

Obviously there were other, less gentle methods of banishing sickness. The Charm 'For a sudden stitch' (*Wið F æ rstice)* (Grendon 1909: 165 Charm A1) begins with typically heathen instructions, in this case to boil together feverfew, red nettle and plantain in butter.

Next follows a long narrative introduction , 'Loud they were, O Loud, when o'er the hill they rode,' presumably referring to the entities responsible for the stitch. This is a very vivid charm, rich in poetic imagery, and with a strong sense of performance.

After telling the patient to '...shield thyself that thou this onslaught mayst survive!' the charm sets out the method of dealing with disease demons thus:

'Neath linden I stood, a light shield beneath,

Where mighty dames their potent arts prepared

And sent their whizzing spears.
Another will I send them back:

A flying arrow right against them.'

Here the spell-caster turns back the magical weapons (spears) and we can only guess at the gestures involved. Possibly the linden tree was considered the safest place to shelter when suffering an attack by the 'stitch.' Alternatively this may have been where the spell was actually performed.

The next line is the basic spell formula, repeated three times (once as a variation) during the spell, '*Out, little spear, if herein it be!*' Even after so many centuries the command retains its sense of excitement and power.

In the original Anglo Saxon this command was written, '*Ut, lytel spere, gif hēr inne s ȳ!*' 'Ut' was one of the earliest magical words I was ever taught, and I still find it useful whenever something has to be banished. (I was always taught to pronounce it to rhyme with 'put'.)

The next part of the same charm refers to a smith, possibly Wayland although he is not named:

'Sat the smith, forged his little knife

...with iron blows sore wounded.

Out, little spear, if herein it be!'

Although the charm does not mention it specifically until the end, the spell caster requires a knife at this point, perhaps to hammer or strike it, as the blacksmith would have hammered while forging. It is not entirely clear from the charm whether the knife represents the 'little spear' or a weapon against the 'little spear.' And as if one smith is not enough, the spell continues,

'Six smiths sat, war spears they wrought.

Out, spear, not in, spear!'

As the spell builds to its climax, the spell-caster boasts of his power to intimidate the disease-demon. There is no attempt to flatter or persuade in this spell, only raw confrontation and aggression:

'If herein be aught of iron, work of witches, it shall melt!'

Such boasts form a large part of the spell, and it must have been extremely impressive when it was performed:

'Wert thou shot in skin, or were shot in flesh,

Or wert shot in blood, or wert shot in bone,

Or wert shot in limb, may ne'er thy life be scathed!

If it were shot of gods, or it were shot of elves,

Or it were shot of hags, now thee I'll help.'

Here the charm gives a list of possible assailants that includes gods, elves and hags or witches, possibly in a descending scale of power. The Anglo-Saxon original uses the word *esa*, (*Gif hit wære ēsa gescot, oððe hit wære ylfa gescot*) possibly from *os*, meaning a god. Some translations equate *esa* with the Aesir, who are usually associated with the Norse tradition. However we cannot take it for granted that *esa* meant the same thing to the Anglo-Saxons.

Having covered all the bases as it were, the spell-caster energetically begins to accompany the words with actions. Even though the charm does not specify what these were, it is likely that every time he said 'This' he must have struck something, perhaps with his knife.

This for relief from shot of gods, this for relief from shot of elves,

This for relief from shot of hags: thee will I help.

Finally the disease demon is dispatched,

Yonder to the mountain flee (hag, who sent the dart]!

Be hale in head! Help thee Lord!

In Anglo Saxon charms it was common to banish disease demons to mountains and hills. The ambiguous final appeal to the 'Lord' suggests an ambiguous replacement for the original heathen deity. This could have been almost any of the Anglo-Saxon pantheon, although Frey in particular was often referred to as 'Lord.'

Chapter Nineteen

Numbers and Elves

T

hree is a significant number in Anglo Saxon healing charms although the way it is used can vary. Sometimes the whole charm has to be said or sung three times, sometimes it is just a single word. Sometimes three figures are invoked. These are have usually been Christianised by the time the charm is transcribed, although originally they may have been deities or heroes from Anglo Saxon myth and legends, or even the Wyrd Sisters. Of course this is not unique to the Anglo-Saxons, and three (together with its multiples especially nine and sometimes twelve) can be found in many cultures including Celtic, Norse and Greco-Roman.

Although the significance of the number three predates Christianity, it was easily assimilated by the early Christian Church because of its links with the Trinity. The number three also appears in several famous Christian stories, including the 'Three Marys' (the Virgin Mary, Mary Magdalen and Mary Cleophas); the Three Wise Men; the three temptations of Christ; the three denials of Christ by Peter; and the three days between Christ's crucifixion and resurrection.

However Christianising the Anglo-Saxon charms did not completely solve the problem and the early Church remained suspicious of any depiction of three identical human figures because of their strong associations with earlier pagan/heathen beliefs and tritheism in particular. The Eastern Orthodox Church however equated three human figures with Abraham's three angelic visitors in Genesis 18:1-8 (Rowlatt 2001:204)

The influence of the number three persisted well into the Middle Ages, particularly in healing. Three different ingredients in a potion entitled it to be called a remedy – the very name suggesting it would be more successful than a mere potion! Drinks or salves were often directed to be applied or taken either three times a day or for three days, and magicians were told to spit three times while performing a charm, or to boil the ingredients three times (Storms, 1948:97).

However, the number three could also be associated with the devil. This may have been an attempt by the Church to show that the devil worked by imitating magic, particularly magic with roots in pre-Christian traditions. Thus it was sometimes claimed that people would die three days after being touched by a demon or spirit, or that a crossroads where three roads met was an evil place, while a gallows would stand on just three legs (Schimmel 1993: 75). Indeed, fear of crossroads had become intense by the late eighth century. According to William of Malmesbury's *De gestis regum Anglorum, ii. 122,* when King Alfred ordered golden armlets to be suspended where public high roads intersected, nobody was prepared to steal them!

Number Nine

Although the number nine is the square of three (3 x 3), sometimes it has its own, unique significance. For example, children had to be baptized within nine nights and Chaney (1962:166) regards this as demonstrating that nine was associated with 'payment for life.

Nine also appears in the Anglo-Saxon trials by ordeal. In trials by carrying a hot piece of iron for example, the distance was the measure of nine of the accused's own feet. The larger the accused's feet, the further he had to walk!

Nine was also used in the trial by the ordeal of eating bread and cheese. After the Normal Conquest in the late 11th century, the bread not only had to be consecrated, but must also weigh exactly nine *denarii*. Before eating, the accused had to say, 'May I choke on this bread if I do not speak the truth' and it is often thought to be where the saying 'Hard Cheese' (as in 'bad luck') originated.

Using the sign of the Cross

Although nowadays the cross is regarded as a completely Christian symbol, its use predates Christianity by hundreds if not thousands of years. Crosses were used as talismans, and also to mark weapons, tools and even food. It was believed that cutting a cross into bread dough helped ensure it cooked properly. Although this is a perfectly sensible thing to do from a culinary point of view as it enables heat to reach the inner dough more quickly, the Church eventually clamped down on the practice. In 1252 Henry III banned bakers in Essex and Hereford from making this mark, although it still survives in the Easter tradition of Hot Cross Buns (Opie and Tatem 1989: 107).

Elves

Words meaning 'elf' are found in many old north European languages. In Anglo-Saxon it was *ælf*, in Old Norse *álfr*, in Middle High German it was *alp*. There was also a shared belief in elves as bringers of sicknesss and disease across northern Europe. To the Anglo-Saxons, *Ælf* could be a generic term for a range of entities, and at least one charm is against 'elfkind' (A.S. *ælfeynn*) suggesting the Anglo-Saxons recognised at least *some* other beings within the same grouping.

It is even possible the word 'oaf' may be a medieval development from the word 'elf.' (Simpson 2011:79) Although nowadays we would think of an oaf as an uncouth sort of person, at one time it was also applied to changelings left by fairies and elves.

There are also several Anglo-Saxon compound words for elf, e.g.: *wudu-ælfenne* meaning the wood elves, *fældælfen* 'field elves' and *sæ-ælfen* 'sea elves' together with *dunælfen* (which could mean either mountain dwelling or even dark elves), *bergælfen and muntælfen.* At first sight it seems the Anglo-Saxons must have recognised a wid range of different types of elf.

However these compound words often turn up as additions above a line of Latin text. This could mean they were originally intended only as a gloss to translate awkward Greco-Roman concepts, such as *castalides, moides, oreades,nalades, nymphae,* and *dryads.* Possibly the sea and water elves were simply the product of a single scribe's literary imagination as he struggled to translate classical terms in a way his Anglo-Saxon readers could understand.

Elves were often blamed for shooting their arrows or flying venom to harm people and animals although it is not always clear exactly which illnesses were associated with these attacks. Almost any unusual or sudden illness could be described as 'elf-shot.' Elves were thought to have made the small flint arrowheads that sometimes still turn up at prehistoric sites so any illness accompanied by a sharp stabbing pain would also be called 'elf shot.' Curiously however, the later iron arrowheads were claimed to have been made by witches (Lacnunga N.134-5)

Other illnesses were more vague, such as 'elf-disease' (A.S. *ælfādl*) and the rather mysterious 'water-elf-disease'](A.S. *wæter ælfādle*). Although this is sometimes identified as dropsy, the Anglo-Saxons had two specific words for that, *wæter-ādl and wæter-seocnys.* So it is possible that water-elf-disease was something else entirely.

Likewise, a famous Charm against elf hiccups (A.S.*ælfsogotha*) in the Leechbook of Bald (Charm 62) has been identified as anything from anaemia to heartburn (McGowan 2009:118) and even 'elf sucking' which implies that elves behaved like vampires! (Shippey 2004:3)

However, the same charm also attempts to banish the *castalides*, who were not part of Anglo-Saxon tradition at all, but named after the ancient Greek Muses who lived at the fountain of Castalia on Parnassus.   Possibly the inclusion of the *castalides* was influenced by Aldhelm, the late seventh century Christian author who mentions them in his work '*Carmen de virginitate*' (Hall 2007: 81).

Later in that same charm we encounter the command 'expelle diabolum' suggesting that by the time the Leechbook of Bald was written (c. ninth century), elves, *castalides* and demons were all being grouped together and blamed for demonic possession (even if nowadays we would dismiss hiccups as really rather trivial.)

Elves were also associated with sexual temptation. Several charms equate them with the "temptations of the fiend/devil" while a reference to '*þam mannum þe deofol mid hæmð*' can translate as 'the people with whom the devil has sexual relations'(Shippey.2004:3).

Of course we still do not know exactly what the heathen Anglo-Saxons thought about elves. Rather than fearing them, they may actually have held the *ælf* in high regard. The way the word appears in many Anglo-Saxon names, such as Alfred or Ælfred, meaning elf counsel or wisdom seems to support this. Yet even this is ambiguous, and could mean either (magical) knowledge about elves, or having the type of wisdom usually associated with elves.

In much the same way, there is confusion about the word *ælfsīden* which is generally thought to mean 'to work elf magic' although it is not clear whether this means using the type of magic favoured by elves, or using magic that will defeat them. Even the Lacnunge, (28) with its 'holy drink against *ælfsīden*' is not clear whether the threat is magic performed by elves, or a magician performing elf-type magic. The suffix *Siða*, to 'work magic' probably originates in the Indo-European language. (Hall 2007:119)

Similar names include Ælf-wine (Elf-friend) and Ælf-stan (Elf-stone). Even the cleric Ælfric, who preached so remorselessly against heathenism, must have known that his own name literally meant 'elf riches'. The continued use of such names well into the Christian period suggests the term 'elf' was often intended as a compliment and originally could have posed no threat to Christianity. Even the Christian King Æthelwulf of Wessex chose Alfred for the name of his youngest son.

It was also considered a great compliment to describe a woman as looking like an elf (Bates 2003:102) perhaps because elves were iridescent and bright. This idea persisted well into the Middle Ages, where Chaucer's Wife of Bath in the Canterbury Tales, mentions an 'elf-queene with her joly compaignye.' The world *ælfsc ȳ ne* means 'elf beautiful' although it also has implications of treachery and enchantment too (Hall 2007:92).

Indeed the Anglo Saxon for a swan is *ylfetu*, with '*ylf*' meaning 'elf white', while *ælf* also means bright and shining. It might even explain how the snow covered Alps in northern Europe got their name! Although the concept of elf-shot is ancient and widespread, more negative aspects of the elf became emphasised out of all proportion once the Church began equating them with demons. Thus *ilfig* can mean mad or frantic, meaning that at some point belief changed so that the condition was blamed on an attack by elves. Yet *ylfig* may mean engaged with an elf, which Hall (2007:149) suggests could mean speaking prophetically through divine or demonic forces, a concept about possession that is also found in ancient Greece.

Certain plants were considered particularly effective against elf attacks, e.g. Ælfthone (better known as Enchanter's Nightshade). Instructions for using this are usually at pains to Christianise the plant by bringing it into church, laying it beneath the altar and having nine masses sung over it (Leechbook of Bald, Charms 3 and 62). Whether or not the priest knew what was going on is anybody's guess. Perhaps it was felt that placing herbs in contact with the altar would somehow consecrate them and make them acceptable. It certainly suggests the Anglo-Saxons believed in the magical transference of power and energy.

Sometimes the same herbs turn up in charms from different traditions. For example, the Anglo-Saxons often used betony to deal with nocturnal goblins and bad dreams. Yet it was also used in Welsh charms to prevent dreaming (Bonser 1926 :360). Although the Anglo Saxons and Welsh were often sworn enemies it is possible there was some sharing of herbal and magical recipes especially in border areas where they would have lived in close proximity. Alternatively the use of betony could belong to some earlier Indo-European tradition that was a common ancestor of both.

Elf-dock (or Elf-wort) is another name for elecampane or helenium, while elf-grass is '...a kind of grass yerbwives find, and give to cattle they conceive injured by elves' (Bonser 1926:358 footnote 37) although the precise type of grass is impossible to identify. We may not know exactly how the heathen Anglo-Saxons regarded elves, yet they remained an important part of cultural consciousness for many centuries.

Chapter Twenty

Plants

A

lthough the heathen Anglo-Saxon period is often referred to as the Dark Ages, medically at least, this term should really be applied to the post-conversion period. Once England – and Europe for that matter – became Christian, most earlier medical knowledge was condemned. By the late tenth/early eleventh century, the Church right across Northern Europe prohibited the collection of medicinal herbs using any incantations other than the Creed and the Lord's Prayer. This suggests not only that plants were once gathered using heathen charms, but also that people were still following the ways of their ancestors.

Church edicts can unwittingly provide us with information about how plants were being used before and during the Conversion of England although many edicts were issued on the continent and not in England. Nevertheless they affected the whole Church, of which Anglo-Saxon England had become a part. Just as the Church was 'catholic' in the sense of being universal, so its edicts affected everyone, not just the area where they were originally issued.

So although edicts can tell us a great deal about *what* was going on, unfortunately we rarely hear exactly where these things were happening. The best we can do is to try and link them to what we can discover about magical practices in Anglo-Saxon England. Much of this seems to have survived for centuries in local folklore, but obviously this can be controversial because (a) we cannot prove unbroken links through these oral traditions and (b) we cannot be sure they were Anglo-Saxon in the first place. Even so, the edicts can make fascinating reading.

For example, in 452CE at the Second Council of Arles, the Church passed a decree prohibiting burning lights near trees, rocks, crossroads and springs. Any Bishop who allowed it to continue was to be excommunicated (Evans-Wentz 1911: 427) We can deduce several things from this, not least the implication that senior clergy had to be threatened in order to make them enforce the decree. Far from swiftly putting a stop to things – as we might expect - they must have been turning a blind eye, probably all over Europe. As we have already seen, many of the English clergy were engaged to some extent in healing and magic. Obviously heathen beliefs did not depart meekly.

Another thing this decree tells us is that people were burning lights in places they considered sacred, which included trees. The decree does not say whether people actually worshipped the trees, nor how they viewed them. We do not know whether they thought trees were gods for example, only that they burned lights nearby. Yet although the information is limited, what it does tell us is that trees continued to be important in some spiritual sense. Not only were ordinary people reluctant to abandon their traditional practices, but also some Christian bishops seemed condone this.

Against this view however, is the fact that this decree was passed in the fifth century, a time when Anglo Saxon England was still mostly heathen. Surely some opposition was only to be expected? Well, yes, but even by the late eighth/early ninth century, heathen beliefs and practices were still so firmly entrenched (in Europe at least) that the Emperor Charlemagne issued a similar edict, stating, 'With respect to trees, stones, and fountains, where certain foolish people light torches or practise other superstitions, we earnestly ordain that that most evil custom... wherever it be found, should be removed and destroyed.' (Boretius 1883 c1.59)

Although Charlemagne did not rule England, he certainly conquered and forced the European Saxons to convert to Christianity. This edict would surely have been issued with the Church's approval and suggests widespread resistance to Christianity along with the persistence of some popular heathen practices. Although tempting to assume these were European rather than English practices, in the eleventh century, King Canute of England was still trying to legislate against very much the same problem (Evans-Wentz

1911:428).

Eventually Church seems to have been forced to assimilate more than it originally intended especially with regard to practices such as burning candles and incense. Anything that could not be eradicated was eventually brought within the Church's control so the authorities could keep an eye on it. People might have been stopped from burning lights near trees, but now they burned them inside the church instead. While this was fine with candles, plants are more difficult to control. We cannot get rid of them all nor tell them where to grow.

However, some early missionaries appear to have tried to do just that. Their prime targets were those trees, especially oaks, that had once been venerated as sacred. In Germany St Boniface smashed up Donar's sacred oak (Donar is usually regarded as a Germanic equivalent of the Anglo-Saxon Thunor), while elsewhere Christian missionaries felled what they called 'god oaks' to prevent people worshipping them. However memory of sacred groves lives on in English place names such as Thunderley and Thundersley in Essex which both mean 'Thunor's grove.'

Pear trees were another target. Its fruit were roughly female-shaped, its wood usually flesh coloured after seasoning, and several European cultures used it in fertility rituals. This shows that initially at least, people were not afraid to approach it. Soon however, rumours spread that demons hid in the branches of pear trees, while witches met beneath them and danced around their trunks at midnight. Possibly this is a folk memory of some early heathen ritual. Although in Germania and France, early missionaries were busy pulling up, chopping down and burning pear trees on the orders of their local bishops, there is no written evidence the same happened in Anglo-Saxon England. Of course it is still possible there were isolated incidents rather than a full-scale campaign against sacred trees.

Like the pear, the apple also suddenly fell from popularity across northern Europe with the coming of Christianity. There is a widespread connection in many cultures between apples, fertility, love and immortality. This makes it almost impossible for us to tease out what is Anglo-Saxon from what is not. Perhaps the original imagery derives from much earlier, Indo-European traditions.

The Church demonised the apple by claiming it was the fruit used by the Serpent in the Garden of Eden to tempt Eve and bring about the downfall of all mankind. In fact in Genesis, Chapter 3, the apple is never mentioned by name and could have been almost anything. Even in Anglo-Saxon the word *eapul* or *æppel* was applied to a wide range of fruits.

Since we lack contemporary heathen accounts of how plants were used in magic and ritual, we have to try and reconstruct what we can. For example, at one time ivy (like mistletoe) was banned from Christmas decorations inside churches even though it was one of the few plants to remain green through the winter. Even later, when it was finally allowed into the church, the plant had to be placed in inconspicuous areas for fear of bad luck.

'Bad luck' is a vague yet potent concept. Nobody can agree exactly how it works. For example, one popular belief was that bringing ivy indoors caused sickness in the household even if it was carried in accidentally on the firewood. Another tradition was that ivy should be kept well away from the mantelpiece and hearth at Yule.

Given that both Yule and Christmas are celebrated around the winter solstice, it suggests that ivy was once used in domestic rituals during December. Possibly it represented the returning sun or springtime because its green leaves promised a new, fertile year ahead. Although this theory cannot be proved, if ivy was never brought indoors and placed around the hearth at Yule, there would be no need to tell people *not* to do it!

Ivy – unlike holly – was traditionally regarded as female. Stories about ivy causing bad luck might therefore have been encouraged in order to weaken women's magical influence in the home so that people would, in St Eligius' words, 'Trust only to the mercy of god'. Of course, none of this proves that *Anglo-Saxon* women carried armfuls of ivy indoors with the intention of decorating the Yule-tide hearth. It may even have been a pre-existing tradition that was adopted by the Anglo-Saxons. Attempts to suppress the practice however suggest it must have had some heathen religious links that were still current during – and after - the Conversion period.

Perhaps the greatest problem the early Church faced was not what people did in public, because after all, that was easy to control. What concerned them most was what people did in private and where they did it.   The various edicts etc., show that heathens often celebrated rituals out of doors, and if these areas were remote, then it would be difficult to keep all of them under observation. Private household shrines were virtually impossible to regulate and control. The answer therefore was to demonise anything connected with such rituals.

The Mother-Die Plants

The 'Mother-Die' plants are a good example of this. These were plants that were supposed to be so unlucky to bring indoors that if you broke the taboo your mother would soon die, hence the nickname. Most, but not all of these plants are white with small flowers, and apart from one or two (e.g. hemlock) are not poisonous. In fact several are popular culinary herbs such as parsley or chervil and turn up in Anglo Saxon charms. Parsley was even used to make a 'holy salve' (Lacnunga No 63) while chervil is used in the famous Nine Herbs Charm (although occasionally it is translated as thyme.)   This Charm is unique in that is mentions Woden by name, so perhaps it was little wonder that the plant – like the god - was ultimately demonised!

Hemlock's Anglo-Saxon names include *wodewistle,* although given that it is *extremely* poisonous, it's unlikely that anyone tried to make a viable instrument from the plant. However since *wod* means fury, it might mean a whistle that brought on a kind of madness or rage, and hemlock poisoning does affect the nervous system. Alternatively, it might be associated with the wilder aspects of Woden.

However, many Mother-Die plants also had strong links with thunder and snakes both of which were associated with the god Thunor. We do not know exactly how his cult was celebrated in England. It may even have varied from one place to another, but it seems likely there was a major festival dedicated to him, perhaps in early summer or late spring when the 'Mother-Die' flowers first bloomed. Given the later prohibition on picking them it seems likely the early heathen rituals must have involved picking and bringing them indoors.

If this theory is correct (and it *is* just a theory), then the early Christian Church demonised certain plants to try and suppress a private aspect of Thunor's cult. One effective way of doing would be to claim that the plants actually caused the very thing they were supposed to avoid. So 'Mother-Die plants' caused women to die, whereas perhaps the original ritual was intended to protect her, or promote fertility.

Many of these 'Mother-Die' plants are covered in tiny white flowers and magically speaking, an abundance of anything symbolises fertility. Of course, fertility was not just about having children; it could refer to making crops grow, hens lay, and ensuring that livestock produced plenty of healthy offspring. Thunor's role as bringer of rain and thunder would have been another link with fertility, since plants need rain in order to grow.

Individual plants offer us further clues. Although the wood anemone was never referred to as Mother-Die, it was considered unlucky if you brought it indoors and in particular would cause someone in the house to die. Its north European nicknames, Devil's Flower, Devil's Claws and Witches Flowers all suggest it had been demonised at some point (De Cleene 2003:48-9). However in England wood anemone was nicknamed Thunderbolt, because picking it caused thunderstorms. This again suggests links with Thunor, especially since so many demonised plants are associated with thunderstorms.

Of course the idea of bringing plants indoors returns us to the question of whether magic functioned differently in a building rather than out of doors. Possibly it was felt that certain types of magic were best performed within the home, or even that one was more susceptible to magic indoors. This may actually have helped the process of demonization with its prohibitions on taking flowers into the home.

We know – because many Mother-Die plants were listed without comment in the Anglo-Saxon herbals - that they were probably not demonised at the time the herbals were written circa the 10th century CE. This suggests that demonization came later, and was intended to deliberately deter people from using certain plants at home for magical (including protective and healing) rituals.

Hawthorn is another Mother-Die plant. Traditionally regarded as feminine, in early summer it is covered in tiny white flowers, possibly a symbol of fertility. Its popular nickname is 'May' perhaps a link with the Celtic festival of Beltane celebrated on the 1st May and famous for its fertility rituals. By the Middle Ages 'Greene hawthorne' had become a metaphor for sex, another clue that its original use was in fertility magic and rituals.

We should not be surprised to find Celtic, Roman and Anglo-Saxon traditions overlapping like this. After all, hawthorn grew just as well among the Anglo-Saxons as it did among the Celts! The Celtic and Germanic people had several shared beliefs including the view that flowers, trees, stars and water had a soul. In many Germanic countries the month of May was celebrated as the time when Woden returned from honeymoon, and people often set up altars decorated with flowers and plants (De Cleene 2003 Vol 2: 19). All these beliefs could combine so that similar rituals were practised by different cultures during the month of May.

In some respects, hawthorn is an unlikely Mother-Die plant. It was used in cures for 'a devil and for madness' (Leechbook of Bald 64; 67) and its leaves and berries are edible. Well into the twentieth century, country children ate the very young green leaves (popularly known as 'bread and cheese') in spring. This was a time when other vitamin-filled greens were in short supply and so hawthorn was a valuable addition to the diet. People even placed small sprays of hawthorn over cots to protect against enchantment.

This poses an interest question: if hawthorn could magically protect a helpless infant then why was it – as a Mother-Die plant - thought capable of killing the mother? Presumably the Mother-Die rumours came later and were intended to deter women (especially those who were pregnant or already had children) from using the plant in private rituals at home. Some however, persisted in using a traditional remedy to protect their children.

There are some other puzzles too. Wild carrot and cow parsley (both Mother-Die plants) were thought to attract snakes although there is no physical explanation for this. Snakes however were also associated with Thunor. So possibly the real reason these plants were demonised was because of their associated with this earlier, heathen deity.

Parsley is another curious Mother-Die plant. Notoriously slow to germinate, folklore attributed this to its need to return nine times (notice the magical number) to the devil. In German witch trials the devil was often called Peterling, which is uncannily close to the Latin name for parsley, Petroselinium (De Cleene 2003 :87). This could suggest that at some time the plant was associated with heathen deities.

Another explanation is that, like rosemary, parsley is said to grow best where the wife is the dominant partner. From this it could be inferred that the plant was at one time associated with female deities. It could well have been used in fertility magic and ritual since not only was it an aphrodisiac (just sowing parsley seeds was thought to make a girl pregnant) but children were often told they were 'born' by being dug out of a parsley patch. Some traditions even claim this was done with a golden spade – a magical touch if ever there was one!

Although as a general rule, most Mother-Die plants have white flowers, there are two important exceptions: rosebay willow herb and red campion. Both are a very bright shade of pink, both were nicknamed 'Thunderflower' and both were believed to cause storms. Immediately this suggests a link with Thunor. In support of this, one of Red Campion's popular names in Welsh is *blodyn neidr*, meaning Snakeflower. Although the Anglo-Saxons do not seem to have associated red campions with snakes, their word for an adder was *nœddre*, which is curiously close to the Welsh *neidr*.

At this point it is tempting to speculate that the heathen Anglo-Saxons had their own version of the Norse legends of Thunor's struggles against the Midgard Serpent. However, in the Nine Herbs Charm it is not Thunor who is fighting the 'wyrm' or dragon (another name for serpent) but Woden, suggesting perhaps a completely different, now lost legend or tradition.

The early Church seems to have taken a dim view of healing the sick. In England, Abbot Ælfric of Eynsham ordered, 'He who is infirm let him pray to the Lord for his healing and patiently endure the pangs... No person must enchant plants with spells but must bless them with God's words'(Meaney 1989). This indicates that the Church regarded healing as an almost exclusively heathen activity at that time. It was only much later that some monasteries began caring for the sick.

At one time it was believed that the heathen Anglo-Saxons knew very little about the treatment of diseases and wounds. However, the various herbals show they were familiar with a range of familiar problems, together with a few (such as worm blisters) that we might not recognise nowadays.

Also, Anglo-Saxon records rarely criticise leeches or healers, nor do there seem to have been laws designed to curtail their practice or specifically punish them if things went wrong and their patient died. This suggests that most healers were considered good at what they did and were valued by their communities.

Whatever the realities of healing, by the time the Anglo-Saxon Charms were written down, a deliberate decision had been made to Christianise them so they were more acceptable to the Church authorities. Whether these changes only happened at the time of transcribing the formulae, or whether they had already been changing for some time before they were written down, we cannot be sure.

Demonising Plants

However, the early Church soon discovered how difficult it is to get rid of something so well established. In particularly, anyone who is ill (not to mention their friends and relatives) will try almost anything for a cure, especially if they believe it works. Faced with this attitude, the early Church had two options, either to use a plant to actively promote Christianity, or to demonise it.

The first method worked best when there was some obvious way of connecting it to a saint or biblical story. For example, a cross-shaped mark on the bottom of a juniper berry could be used as an aid when preaching about the Crucifixion. A dark mark on the leaf of *Polygonium persicaria*, was explained as 'Our Lady's Thumbprint,' while *Alchemilla mollis* became known as Lady's Mantle.   We cannot be certain when these nicknames were first given, nor by whom, and nobody now remembers what the original heathen names were.

The second option, demonization, was used for plants that could not be Christianised. Again, we find clues in plant names. For example, both southernwood and rosemary were known in some areas as 'Old Man'; Traveller's Joy or Wild Clematis were called 'Old Man's Beard' while meadowsweet was sometimes called 'Old Man's Pepper'. But who or what was the 'Old Man'? Possibly the name referred to a heathen deity that was later demonised as the Devil.   In Anglo-Saxon the word 'man' can have a variety of meanings; when written as *'màn'* it can mean wicked or sinful (Bosworth 1838:229).

The demonization of rosemary is particularly interesting because folk tradition always claimed that it grew best wherever 'the old grey mare was the better horse' This is usually taken to mean wherever the wife ruled the husband. It is possible therefore that rosemary was sacred to a pre-Christian goddess, although we do not know whether this was an Anglo-Saxon, Celtic, Roman or even earlier deity.

The rowan tree was another victim of demonization, although it remained popular in protective folk magic where it was also used as a Rod of Life plant. Touching a person or animal with a wand or rod of rowan was thought to bestow fertility and life on them. An alternative name for rowan was quickbeam, which derives from the Anglo-Saxon *'cweoc'* or *'cwic'* meaning 'alive' (as opposed to dead, hence the saying, 'the quick and the dead').

Pregnant women still sometimes say they feel the baby 'quicken' meaning they feel it kicking, a sure sign (back in the days before ultrasound scans) that it was still alive. Other contenders for the name of quickbeam include wych elm and even juniper.

Rowan also has strong links with Thor, and in northern Europe was nicknamed Thor's Protector or Thor's Helper. There may have been a now lost Anglo-Saxon equivalent too. Right into the nineteenth century, people would tie red threads in its branches to protect against witchcraft both in England and Northern Europe.

A spoon made from rowan or quickbeam was recommended for stirring a healing potion in the Lacnunga (Charm No 31) This indicates how the Anglo-Saxons believed that everyday objects could be empowered by the materials from which they were made and could transfer this power to anything they touched.   Likewise the reverse was true, and diseases could be transferred from the patient to the spoon (Grendon 1909:130).

The Church's lack of interest in any sort of healing other than prayer meant that even plants with powerful medicinal properties, such as the elder, were routinely demonised. By the late Middle Ages the tree was considered so dangerous that people were frightened to walk past it at night! It was also believed that an 'Old Hag' lived in elder trees, and people refused to burn its wood on the fire because they feared the 'Old Lady' would come and sit on top of their chimney.

In Germanic areas of Europe the elder was referred to as 'Frau Holle' while in England, those who still used the tree in folk medicine, treated it with the greatest respect, asking permission to pick its flowers and berries from the 'Old Gal' or 'Mother Elder.' It seems clear the female entity living in the tree was some sort of goddess, possibly known as Frau Holle, Holda, Hulda, Old Gal, Mother Elder or some now forgotten name. In Anglo-Saxon the Elder was known as *ellen* meaning power or strength, and this remained a popular girl's name right up into the twentieth century.

Another possibility is that Old Woman or Old Gal originated from the Anglo-Saxon words *galdor* (a charm) or *gal* whose meanings include lusty, wanton and wicked. Possibly therefore the original deity was a fertility goddess, eventually demonised by the early Church who used the word *wyrtgalstre* meaning a plant-charmer to describe witches. (Pollington 2003:469)

It was often claimed that an elder tree made nearby water undrinkable. It is certainly a thirsty plant, often growing near springs and wells. Yet these are both places where, according to early Church authors, heathen rituals persisted. So it is quite possible that the rumour was started to discourage people from using their need to gather water as an excuse for visiting sacred wells or springs.

Elder certainly seems to have held a special place in the hearts of the heathen Anglo-Saxons. In England in 970CE, almost a century before the Battle of Hastings, but already well into the Christian Anglo-Saxon period, King Edgar banned the 'idle use' of the Elder and other trees, a clear indication of the difficulties in eradicating tree veneration (Cambrian Archaeological Association 1863:226). Other superstitions, that sleeping under an elder or even sitting in its shade on warm evenings could kill you, suggest that originally the tree played an important role in summer rituals.

Unlike Elder, Flax managed to escape demonization, even though it was sacred to several heathen goddesses in northern Europe including the Norse fertility goddess Freya and the Germanic goddesses Holle or Holda. An entity known as the Lady of the Flax was believed to live amongst the linen in the home suggesting she was as a household spirit or deity. In Norse tradition, Freya's team of cats had reins of flowering flax stems and she is often depicted spinning (De Cleene 2003 Vol 2:233). However there is no obvious surviving trace of this imagery in Anglo-Saxon art or poetry.

The tradition that flax should be sown on a Thursday suggests a link with Thunor. Possibly this god was thought to influence all living things, and it was certainly believed that plants, such as mushrooms were at their best on Thursdays. The Anglo-Saxons named at least one plant, the *Ðunor wyrt*, after Thunor. This is thought to be a houseleek, a plant believed to protect the home against being struck by lightning.

Flax was also associated with hair as in the the Old English 'flix', and blonde hair is often called 'flaxen.' In Austria the flax plant was actually called *haar*. In England the blue flax flowers were associated with love and fertility, and in order to attract these properties, brides traditionally wore 'something blue.' Flax's close association with fertility can be seen in the belief that only a naked woman could sow it. In some areas it was also the custom for women to wander naked in the flax fields on St John's Eve, around the Summer Solstice.

In Somerset there was a folk tradition that people should wear something blue on the first day of the flax harvest (Baker 1996:60). This sounds very much like the remnants of a fertility ritual. In particular it echoes the old 'something old, something new, something borrowed, something blue' tradition at weddings, which were always a good occasion for fertility traditions. Also the 'just as... so may' principle is at work here. Magically wearing blue makes the statement, 'Just as I am covered in blue, so may this field be covered in blue flax flowers'.

However, we have to be careful not to read too much into this. Although the Anglo-Saxons eventually settled in Somerset (AS *Somersæte*) which eventually became part of the Kingdom of Wessex, this did not happen until *after* the conversion to Christianity. Also there is evidence of earlier Celtic and Roman settlements in the area so perhaps the new settlers borrowed earlier traditions and adapted them for their own use. Alternatively, this may have been a long-standing Anglo-Saxon tradition which was brought into Somerset with the new settlers. The sad truth is that we may never be certain.

Flax is also associated with movement magic, involving dancing and rolling, all suggestive of ancient fertility rites particularly those of the Anglo-Saxons and other peoples of northern Europe (De Cleene 2003, Vol 2: 239) Originally the Church tolerated the tradition of dancing during field and harvest celebrations, although once nuns were reported dancing in a church, Theodore's Penitential (Paragraph 38.9) promptly forbade it!

On the face of it therefore, flax should have been a prime candidate for demonization. It was after all, one of the oldest plants to be cultivated by the Indo-Europeans, and with its many small seeds was an obvious ingredient in protective and fertility magic. What ultimately saved flax from the elder's fate, was the fact it yielded high quality linen which the Church used for its vestments. So flax was duly put to ecclesiastical use and the Church continued a heathen tradition of wearing ritual linen robes made of flax.

Other Plant Remedies

Childbirth and the days following it were particularly hazardous for women. The Anglo-Saxons recommended eleven or thirteen grains of coriander, placed in a linen cloth; these were believed to induce a quick birth, but only if they were held on the woman's left thigh by a virgin (Old English Herbarium No 104).

Although the virgin's gender is not specified, it seems unlikely that a young male would have been present at a birth. In the East, coriander had been used for centuries to relieve menstrual and labour pain, perhaps due to its high content of volatile oils. Whether the Anglo-Saxons were aware of its physical properties we do not know, but the inclusion of a specific number of seeds and the requirement for a virgin to handle these suggests a combination of magical and physical methods.

Another magical herb remedy is found in the Leechbook of Bald where a charm to counter visits by nocturnal entities recommend binding up 'lupine and garlic and betony and frankincense' in a fawn skin (Leechbook 1.60 Grendon 1909: 136 charms D1 and D2). Although translators often suggests the entity in question is an incubus, the original Anglo-Saxon, *'Gif mon mare r ī de,'* suggests it was in fact the Night Mare, (sometimes also called 'The Hag'). This tries to choke, press or stifle the victim and similar entities occurs world-wide. Some people suffer only one attack in a lifetime, others have them regularly. One thing most victims agree upon is that the attacks are terrifying and the memory of them persists for months if not years.

Like many other cultures, the Anglo-Saxons made use of the mandrake. In the Old English Herbarium (Charm 132.6), mandrake placed in the middle of the house was used to force out evil. The instructions for digging up the plant are very similar to those found elsewhere in the Graeco-Roman Empire. Traditionally dogs were used to drag the mandrake out of the ground since it would scream as it was being removed, and the sound would kill whoever was responsible. However the Anglo-Saxon version only promises darkly that the dog will be 'betrayed in the same way'.

Part of the power of the mandrake lay in its supposed resemblance to the human figure. Another plant with similar properties was the sea holly. According to the Old English Herbarium (Charm 182), it had a head like a gorgon, while its twigs had the eyes and a nose like a snake. Mention of the gorgon immediately suggests Greco-Roman influence, although snakes are common to many traditions, including the Anglo-Saxons. Like the mandrake it was important to gather sea holly correctly, using iron, avoiding direct sunlight and never looking at the entire root while digging it out. It was considered a great protector against evil.

Sometimes special prayers were recommended for certain types of herb gathering. These included the *Benedictio herbarum* (for herbs), *Benedictio potus* (for medicines) and the *Benedictio unguentum* (for salves). Possibly these were a replacement for earlier Anglo-Saxon heathen formulae.

Although it is impossible to reconstruct precisely what heathen plant gatherers were actually doing, very occasionally we do catch a fleeting glimpse of Anglo-Saxon ritual. Even if it is not complete enough for us to be certain, it is certainly enough to make us pause and wonder.

For example, an instruction to take celandine root out of the ground 'with the two hands turned upwards,' corresponds with the traditional heathen prayer position, sitting with the palms of the hands turned upwards on the knees (Chaney 1970:116). This suggests that gathering plants for potions etc., originally formed part of a heathen religious ritual. The substitution of paternosters etc., as the charms were Christianised therefore makes perfect sense. However, we cannot know how much magical content was removed from the charms *before* they were written down.

For example, a charm to cure painful eyes (OE Herbarium No 19) recommends going to a knotgrass or *blódwyrt* plant, explaining why you intend to gather it and then marking around it with a golden ring. Note here that permission to gather was not being requested, simply stating the intention was enough. This suggests that Anglo-Saxon leeches may have viewed themselves as working in magical partnership with herbs and plants. Alternatively it may have been felt their training (and we do not know exactly what this entailed) gave them magical authority over plants etc., so that permission did not need to be sought.

The seeds of the castor-oil plant were valued for averting storms at sea, hailstorms and lightning bolts, suggesting the Anglo-Saxons practised weather magic. Bede (EHEN Chapter 15) describes how St Aidan gave a phial of holy oil to a priest named Utta, telling him to use it to calm a storm at sea. Centuries earlier, the Roman author Pliny the Elder had written about using oil to calm the water, showing how this was a widespread magical practice, although we do not know exactly when or where it originated.

However the Anglo-Saxons used the seeds rather than the oil itself, which indicates a magical rather than physical effect upon the storm. In Charm 176, in The Old English Herbarium,. the plant is addressed directly, with an appeal for it to be 'present at my songs' suggesting weather magic was sung or chanted rather than spoken.

The same charm directs that whoever gathers the plant must be clean, ('*clæn*'), a word denoting not only physical cleanliness but also purity, chastity or even someone who has been purified. The scribe must have assumed his readers would understand what was meant and makes no effort to explain further.

Gathering periwinkles (OE Herbarium No 179) also required that the person picking them had to be free from every defilement. Also the plant could only be gathered when the moon was either one, nine, eleven, thirteen and thirty nights old. Given that periwinkle was used for so many different intentions, including possession, snakes, poison, threats and fear, it is possible that a particular moon-phase ruled a specific problem.

A charm against Water Elf Disease (which could apparently be diagnosed by the patient's livid finger nails, watery eyes and a tendency to 'look downwards') recommends steeping various herbs in ale, together with holy water (which may originally have been dew). The Spell-caster or Leech then sings the following over the patient :

Round the wounds I have wreathed the best of healing amulets

That the wounds may neither burn nor burst,

Nor grow worse nor putrefy,

Nor throb, nor be filthy wounds,

Nor cut in deeply; but let him keep the sacred water for himself,

Then it will pain you no more than it pains the land by the sea. (from Grendon 1909:195 Charm B5)

Here we see that the herbs, ale and holy water mixture were placed in a circle around the patient's wounds or sores. Then the Leech appeals 'many times' over the wound: '*May Earth remove you with all her might and main.*' The charm also uses the traditional 'just as... so may' formula, e.g. 'Then it will pain you no more than it pains the land by the sea.'

Running or spring water or even dew was the heathen equivalent of holy water. Ale also appears in many Anglo-Saxon charms. Although we take it for granted nowadays that our water is safe to drink, centuries ago it was often contaminated, either by flax retting, tanning or even by human waste. For most people therefore, drinking water was a risky business and so ale, beer, wine or cider were regarded as safer since the alcohol content (hopefully) killed off a multitude of unpleasant things.

Back in the nineteenth century, my husband's grandfather never drank water until he was twelve years old, because the nearest wells were considered unsafe. Instead he drank cider. Wine was also widely used in the Charms, since like the Romans before them, the Anglo-Saxons cultivated many vineyards (as can be seen in the Domesday Book).

Occasionally we can track a relatively modern folk remedy back into the Anglo-Saxon herbals. For example, the Leechbook of Bald (No. 59) recommends making a poultice from dough to cure an 'inflamed blister.' Even when I was young people used bread poultices (basically bread soaked in very hot water, wrung out and bandaged onto the inflamed area) to draw out pus from wounds and boils.

Leeches

Although nowadays we think of a leech being an unpleasant looking blood sucking creature, in Anglo-Saxon *læce* meant a doctor or physician. Many of these – as we can see in the early herbals – also practised magic along with basic medicine. The word leech turns up in place names, such as Lesbury (Northumberland, Lexham (Norfolk), Latchmere (Surrey, Lashbrooke (Oxfordshire) and Larchford (Cheshire) (Pollington 2003:41).

Leech also turns up in the Anglo-Saxon name for the fourth finger of either hand, (next to the little finger) which was the Leech Finger or *læcefinger*. Even in the ancient Greco-Roman world, it was claimed that this finger had an artery that ran directly to the heart, and may explain why it was chosen for the wearing of wedding rings. Anglo-Saxon healers used that finger for applying salves, and sometimes also for tasting their potions as they brewed.

My own experience of the *læcefinger* came in one of the first exercises I ever learned for detecting energy. Try outstretching your left hand, palm uppermost, and then use the leechfinger of the right hand to trace a line just above the leechfinger of the left. You should feel a slight breeze running along the left-hand finger. As an experiment you can try changing over which hand does the tracing, and use different fingers, but always above the *læcefinger* of one hand. It's quite an interesting little exercise!

We do not know exactly how people trained to use herbs and magic for healing. It may have been hereditary, or perhaps people were chosen on the basis of certain criteria. A certain amount of herb lore was probably passed down orally in families and communities, based perhaps on trial and error. We cannot even be sure whether both men and women could be leeches, and if so, whether they specialised in different types of work. Perhaps women were involved in charms to help in conception, pregnancy and birth, and also children's ailments. After all, our word midwife derives from Anglo-Saxon!

There may also have been some specialists who devised, developed and used the information that later was transcribed into the main surviving Anglo-Saxon herbal texts: The Lacnunga, the Old English Herbarium and the Leechbook of Bald. The Leechbook of Bald names four leeches, Oxa, Dun, Bald himself and Cild, who was the book's scribe, all of whom were male.

And Finally…

In the early days when I first started writing this book, Britain was gripped by an unusually bitter winter. Deep snow made travel difficult at best, dangerous at worst. Looking out of my window, my neighbours, their faces hidden, all looked the same, wrapped in the same uniform of hat, coat, gloves and scarf. They barely spoke, just trudged with their heads down against the biting cold. Children shrieked and played for a day or two on improvised sleds of cardboard and plastic bags. But then they too, fell silent as the mountainsides quickly became too slippery to climb back up again.

And this set me thinking about the Anglo-Saxons and their world. They must have known many bitter weathers, too. Living in relatively small communities, they must have dreaded cold winters and the sheer struggle to keep alive. I looked at them with new respect for their self reliance and indeed their confidence in each other too. No wonder heathenism places such strong emphasis on the bonds of friendship and kinship. Without it, life would have been impossible.

As I continued writing I realised I could only ever hope to cover a tiny part of their magical world. I hope I have provided enough food for thought in these pages to encourage you, the reader, to travel on and explore further for yourself.

I do realize that throughout this book I have been rather cautious, pointing out that we cannot be sure about certain things, or that there is little evidence for them. Although I know such caution is frustrating, it also highlights potential pitfalls. The biggest danger with pitfalls is not knowing what they are nor where they lurk. Once we know, we can take steps to avoid them. It is all too easy to rush in with wild claims which we then follow blindly. They are very attractive and we would dearly like to believe them. But they will lead us up dark alleyways and waste valuable time and energy.

Once we understand the weaknesses in such claims however, we can begin looking either for more evidence or other solutions. All the time new discoveries are being made, or new interpretations of older evidence are suggested.

And who knows? Perhaps one day, we *will* find the answers. But meanwhile, the more we learn the more likely we are to at least ask the right questions.

Bibliography and Further Reading
Primary sources

Ælfric, Abbot of Eynsham On the False Gods, in John C. Pope, ed., Homilies of Ælfric: A Supplementary Collection, 2 vols., Early English Text Society 259-260 (London 1967-68) 2: 667-724. Translation by P. Baker Can be read online at :

http://faculty.virginia.edu/OldEnglish/aelfric/defalsis.html

Aelfric, Skeat. W. [trans],(1881) *Aelfric's Lives of Saints : being a set of sermons on saint's days formerly observed by the English Church*, Early English Text Society, Trubner & Co London. Read online at:

http://www.archive.org/stream/aelfriclivesofs01aelfuott/aelfricslivesofs01

Ammianus Marcellinus, *Roman History.*London: Bohn (1862) (Book 16, II:12)

Bede, Jane L.C., [Trans] (1903) *The Ecclesiastical History of the English Nation*, London: J.M. Dent; Can be read online here:

http://www.fordham.edu/halsall/basis/bede-book1.html

Bede, Giles J.A., [trans] (1910) *Life and Miracles of St. Cuthbert*, in *Ecclesiastical History of the English Nation*, Everyman's Library London

Can be read online at :

http://www.fordham.edu/halsall/basis/bede-cuthbert.asp

Bede, Wallis, F. [Trans and Ed] (1999)*The Reckoning of Time*, Liverpool University Press

Bradley, S.A.J. [Trans] (1991) *Anglo Saxon Poetry*, The Everyman Library, Dent

Boretius , (1883, reprinted 1984) *Capitularia region Francorum*, Hahnsche Buchhandlung

Burchard of Worms, The Corrector can be read in McNeill (1933) [see below] and online here:

http://files.meetup.com/262110/Burchard%20of%20Worms's%20Corrector.tx

Gildas, *The Works* (from **Giles, J.A.,** (1891) *Six old English chronicles*, G. Bell & Sons, London can be read online

http://www.fordham.edu/halsall/basis/gildas-full.asp

Nennius: Historia Brittonum, from *Six Old English Chronicles*. ed. **J. A. Giles** (1848) Henry G. Bohn, London. Read online at:

http://www.fordham.edu/halsall/basis/nennius-full.asp

Poetic **Edda** translated by Henry Adams Bellows (1936) can be read online at: http://www.sacred-texts.com/neu/poe/

Sturluson, S., A. Faulkes (Ed.), (1982) *Edda. Prologue and Gylfaginning*, Oxford: Clarendon Press

Tacitus, Mattingly H. [Trans]., (1948) *The Agricola and the Germania,,* Penguin Classics

The Exeter Book, (1936) George Routledge & Sons, Columbia University Press

Kelly, S.E. (Ed) (2001) *Charters of Abingdon Abbey*, 2 vols, Anglo-Saxon Charters, 7–8 Oxford

Secondary sources

Bailey, A.. (1997) *The Caves of the Sun, the origin of Mythology*, Jonathan Cape, London

Baker, M. (1996) *Discovering the Folklore of Plants*, M Baker, Shire Publications Ltd.

Baring-Gould, S. (1913) *A Book of Folklore*, Collins, London

Bates, B., (2003) *The Real Middle-Earth*, Pan Books

Bolton, H.C. (1888)The Counting-out Rhymes of Children. London

Bond, J.M., (1996), Burnt Offerings: Animal Bone in Anglo-Saxon Cremations, *World Archaeology*, Vol. 28, No. 1

Bonser, W., (1946) Anglo-Saxon Laws and Charms Relating to Theft, *Folklore*, Vol. 57, No. 1, pp. 7-11

Bonser W., (1926) Magical Practices against Elves, *Folklore*, Vol. 37, No. 4 (Dec. 31), pp. 350-363

Bosworth, J., (1838) *A Dictionary of the Anglo-Saxon Language: Containing the Accentuation - The Grammatical Inflections - The Irregular Words Referred to Their Themes*, Longman, Rees, Orme, Brown, Green and Longman.

Bourne, H. (1725) *Antiquitates vulgares:* or, the antiquities of the common people. Giving an account of several of their opinions and ceremonies. read on line at:

http://quod.lib.umich.edu/e/ecco/004875177.0001.000/1:1?rgn=div1;view=fulltext

Bradley, J., (Nov. 1990) Sorcerer or Symbol?: Weland the Smith in Anglo-Saxon Sculpture and Verse, *Pacific Coast Philology*, Vol. 25, No. 1/2, pp. 39-48

Bradley, R. (1998) *The Passage ofArms: An Archaeological Analysis of Prehistoric Hoard and Votive Deposits*, Oxford: Oxbow.

Branston, B., 1957, *The Lost Gods of England*, Thames and Hudson, London,

Brentano, R., (ed.), (1964) *The Early Middle Ages: 500-1000*, Sources in Western Civilisation, University of California, Berkeley

Cambrian Archaeological Association (1863) *Archaeologia Cambrensis*

Cameron, K., (1959)*The Place-Names of Derbyshire*, 3 vols, English Place-Name Society, 27–29, Cambridge

Chaney, W. A., (1960) Paganism to Christianity in Anglo-Saxon England, *The Harvard Theological Review*, Vol. 53, No. 3, pp. 197-217

Chaney, W.A. (1962) Aethelberht's Code and the King's Number, *The American Journal of Legal History*, Vol. 6, No. 2 (Apr., 1962), pp. 151-177

Chaney, W.A. (1970) *The Cult of Kingship in Anglo-Saxon England*, Manchester University Press

Chantepie, P. D., (1902) [Trans. from the Dutch by B. J. Vos] *The Religion of the Teutons*, Boston.

Cockayne, O. (1865, reprint 1961) *Leechdoms, Wortcunning, and Starcraft of Early England*, 3 vols. (London, 1865; reprint, 1961),

Conrad, Joseph L. (1983) Magic Charms and Healing Rituals in Contemporary Yugoslavia, *Southeastern Europe* 10 (1983) pp99-120.

Crawford, S., (2004) Votive Deposition, Religion and the Anglo-Saxon Furnished Burial Ritual, *World Archaeology*, Vol. 36, No. 1, The Object of Dedication, pp. 87-102

Davidson, H.R.E., (1963), Folklore and Man's Past, *Folklore*, Vol. 74, No. 4 (Winter), pp. 527-544

Davidson H.R.E., Webster, L., (1967) The Anglo-Saxon Burial (Woodnesborough), at Coombe Kent, *Medieval Archaeology*, Volume 11

Davidson, H.R.E., (1973) *Gods and Myths of Northern Europe*, Penguin Books

Davies, O., (1996) Healing Charms in Use in England and Wales 1700-1950, *Folklore*, Vol. 107 , pp. 19-32

De Cleene, M., Le Jeune, M.C., (2003), *Compendium of Symbolic and ritual plants in Europe*, Vol 1 Man and Culture Publishers, Ghent

Dickins, B., (1915) *Runic and Heroic Poems of the Old Teutonic Peoples*, Cambridge University Press

Earle,J . A., (Ed.) (1888). A Handbook to the Land Charters and Other Saxonic Documents. Oxford: Clarendon Press.

Esmonde-Cleary, A.S.(1991), *The Ending of Roman Britain*, Routledge

Evans-Wentz, W.Y. (1911) *The Fairy Faith in Celtic Countries*, read online at: http://www.sacred-texts.com/neu/celt/ffcc/index.htm

Fry, D. K., (1971) 'Wulf and Eadwacer' : A Wen Charm, *The Chaucer Review*, Vol. 5, No. 4, pp. 247-263

Fuller, S.D., (1980) Pagan Charms in Tenth-Century Saxony? The Function of the Merseburg Charms, *Monatshefte*, Vol. 72, No. 2 (Summer), pp. 162-170

Gardner, G.B. (1942) British Charms, Amulets and Talismans, *Folklore*, Vol. 53, No. 2 (Jun.)

Geake, H. (1997)*The Use of Grave Goods in Conversion Period England, c. 600-850*, Oxford: British Archaeological Reports British Series 261

Gelling, M. (1961) Place Names and Anglo-Saxon Paganism, *University of Birmingham Historical Journal* 8, 7-25

Godfrey-Faussett, B. (1856) Inventorium Sepulchrale, London

Gordon, R.K. (1926) *Anglo-Saxon Poetry*, London

Goody, J., (1983) *The Development of the Family and Marriage in Europe*, Past and Present Publications, Cambridge

Grattan, J.H.G., (1927) Three Anglo-Saxon Charms from the 'Lacnunga', *The Modern Language Review*, Vol. 22, No. 1, pp. 1-6

Grendon, F., (1909) The Anglo-Saxon Charms, *The Journal of American Folklore*, Vol. 22, No. 84 (Apr. - Jun.,)pp. 105-237 read online: http://archive.org/details/anglosaxoncharms00gren

Grimm, J., (1842   ) *Deutsche Mythologie*, Göttingen) (Modern reprint *Teutonic Mythology*, published 2004 by Dover Publications)

Grinsell, L. (1936) *The Ancient Burial Mounds of England*, Methuen.

Griffiths, B.,1996, Aspects of Anglo-Saxon Magic, Anglo-Saxon Books

Gummere, F. B.(1892) *Germanic Origins*, New York

Haddan, A.W. and **Stubbs, W.,** (1871) *Councils and Ecclesiastical Documents relating to Great Britain and Ireland*, Vol 3, Oxford

Hall, A. (2006) Are there any Elves in Anglo-Saxon Place-Names?
Nomina: Journal of the Society for Name Studies in Britain and Ireland
29:pp. 61-80.

Hall, A., (2007) *Elves in Anglo-Saxon England: Matters of belief, health, gender and identity*, The Boydell Press

Herlihy, D., (1978) 'Medieval Children' in *Essays in Medieval Civilization:The Walter Prescott Webb Memorial Lectures* ed. by B. Lackner and K. Philp, Austin

Hunt, R., (1865 reprinted 1923) *Popular Romances of the West of England*, London, Chatto and Windus,

Hunter-Blair, P. (1976) *Northumbria in the Days of Bede*, London: Gollancz

Hutton, R. (1996) The Stations of the Sun, Oxford University Press

Jolliffe, J. E. A. (1947) *The Constitutional History of Medieval England*, W. W. Norton & Co New York

Krapp G. P., Dobbie E.V.K., (Eds) (1931-53) *The Anglo-Saxon Poetic Records, A Collective Edition,* 6 Vols London and New York

Kuefler, M.S., (1991) *A Wryed Existence': Attitudes toward Children in Anglo-Saxon England, Journal of Social History,* Vol. 24, No. 4, pp. 823-834

Laing, L., Laing J., (1979), *Anglo Saxon England,* Book Club Associates with Routledge and Kegan Paul Ltd.

Lapidge, M., Godden, M., Keynes, S. (Eds), (2007), *Anglo Saxon England,* Volume 33, Cambridge University Press

McGowan, J. (2009), Elves, Elf-shot, and Epilepsy: OE ælfādl, ælfsiden, ælfsogeþa, bræccoþu, and bræcsēoc, *Studia Neophilologica* 81: p116–120

McNeill, J.T., (Oct 1933) Folk-Paganism in the Penitentials, *The Journal of Religion,* Vol. 13, No. 4, pp. 450-466

Magoun Jr, F. P., (1947) On Some Survivals of Pagan Belief in Anglo-Saxon England, *The Harvard Theological Review,* Vol. 40, No. 1, pp. 33-46

Maguire, H., (1997) Magic and Money in the Early Middle Ages, *Speculum,* Vol. 72, No. 4 (Oct., 1997), pp. 1037-1054

Maitland, S.R. (first edition 1841) *The Dark Ages,* London, [the 1844 version can read online at:

http://www.archive.org/details/darkages00maitiala

Mawer, A. (1919) Animal and Personal Names in O.E. Place-Names, *The Modern Language Review,* Vol. 14, No. 3 (Jul.), pp. 233-244

Meaney, A. (1989) *Women, Witchcraft and Magic in Anglo-Saxon England,* in Scragg, D.G. (Ed) *Superstition and Popular Medicine in Anglo-Saxon England,* Manchester University Press

Merrifield, R. (1987) *The Archaeology of ritual and Magic,* Batsford, London

Meyer, E. H., (1903) *Mythologie der Germanen,* Strassburg

Naumann, H., (1938) Die Magische Seite des Altgermanischen Königtums und Ihr Fortwirken in Christlicher Zeit, *Wirtschaft und Kultur.* Festschrift zum 70. Geburtstag von Alfons Dopsch (Baden bei Wien)

Ogden, D. (2009) 2nd edition *Magic , Witchcraft, and Ghosts in the Greek*

and Roman worlds, A Source Book, Oxford University Press

Opie, I. , Tatem, M (1989) A Dictionary of Superstitions. Oxford: Oxford University Press,

Owen G.R. (1981) *Rites and Religions of the Anglo Saxon*, Newton Abbot

Peters H. (1918) Aus der Geschichte der Pflanzenwelt in Wort und Bild, Mittenwald : A. Nemayer

Phythian-Adams, C., (1975) *Local History and Folklore, a New Framework*, London

Pollington, S. (2003) *Leechcraft, Early English Charms, Plantlore and Healing*, Anglo Saxon Books

Pounds, N. J. (1993) *Hearth and Home, a History of Material Culture*, Indiana University Press

Raffel, B. (Trans) (1964, 2nd Edition) *Poems from the Old English*, Lincoln, Nebraska

Richards, J. D. (1987) *The Significance of Form and Decoration of Anglo-Saxon Cremation Urns*, British Archaeological Reports, British Series 166

Robertson, A. J., (Ed.) 1956 [1939]. Anglo-Saxon Charters, Cambridge: Cambridge University Press.

Ross, M.C. (1985) Concubinage in Anglo-Saxon England, *Past & Present*, No. 108 (Aug.), pp. 3-34

Rowlatt, U., (2001) Popular Representations of the Trinity in England, 990-1300, *Folklore*, Vol. 112, No 2., pp. 201-210

Ryan, J.S. (1963) Evidence from the Poetry for a Cult of Woden in Anglo-Saxon England, *Folklore*, Vol. 74, No. 3 (Autumn), pp. 460-480

Schimmel, A. (1993) *The Mystery of Numbers*, Oxford University Press

Shippey, T., (2004) Light-elves, Dark-elves, and Others:

Tolkien's Elvish Problem, *Project Muse*, West Virginia University Press

Simpson, J (1979) The King's Whetstone, *Antiquity*, 53, 96 – 101

Simpson, J (2011) On the Ambiguity of Elves , *Folklore*, Volume 122, No.1, 76-83

Speake, G. (1980) Anglo-Saxon Animal Art and its Germanic Background, Oxford University Press

Stoodley, N., (2000) From the Cradle to the Grave: Age Organization and the Early Anglo-Saxon Burial, *World Archaeology*, Vol. 31, No. 3

Storms, G. (1948) Anglo Saxon Magic, The Hague: Nijhoff

Talbot, C. H. (1954) *the Anglo Saxon Missionaries in Germany*, London and New York

Taylor, P. B., (1983) Searonioas: Old Norse Magic and Old English Verse, *Studies in Philology*, Vol. 80, No. 2, pp. 109-125

Thorpe, B (Ed) (1840) *Ancient Laws and Institutes of England*, 2 vols. London, 1840

Tupper, F. Jr., (1895) Anglo-Saxon Dæg-Mæl, *PMLA*, Vol. 10, No. 2, pp. 111-241

Turner, S. (2006) *Making a Christian Landscape: The countryside in early medieval Cornwall, Devon and Wessex*, University of Exeter Press.

Turner, S. (1836) *History of Anglo-Saxons*, 3 vols. London, 1836.

Turville-Petre, E.O.G.,(1964) *Myth and Religion of the North, the religion of ancient Scandinavia* Weidenfeld and Nicolson, London

Vandersall, A.L., (1972) The Date and Provenance of the Franks Casket, *Gesta*, Vol. 11, No. 2 (1972), pp. 9-26

Wade-Evans, A.W. (1938) *Nennius's 'History of the Britons,'* London

Whitelock, D. (1949) Anglo-Saxon Poetry and the Historian, *Transactions of the Royal Historical Society*, 4th series, xxxi

Whitelock, D. (Ed) (1955) *English Historical Documents c. 500-1042* London

Whitelock, D., (Ed.), (1979) *English Historical Documents, Vol. I*, London,

Whitelock, D., (1986 [1930]) *Anglo-Saxon Wills*, Holmes Beach, Fla.: William W. Gaunt & Sons.

Whitelock, D., (1996) ***English Historical Documents 500-1042*, Routledge**

Wilby, E. (2010) *Cunning Folk and Familiar Spirits*, Sussex Academic Press

Wilson, D.M., (1962) Anglo-Saxon Rural Economy: a survey of the archaeological evidence and a suggestion, *Agricultural History Review* Volume 10 part 2, p65 – 79

Wilson, D. (1992) *Anglo-Saxon Paganism*, London: Routledge.

Zadora-Rio, E. (2003) The making of churchyards and parish territories in the early-medieval landscape of France and England in the 7th–12th centuries: A reconsideration, *Medieval Archaeology* 42: 1-19.